"As chairman of XLN fo............................impressed by the highly focused ....)wth. The senior team, under the_..culture of continuous improvement, 'pulling up trees' in the pursuit of excellence and customer service along this growth path. It is remarkable how XLN has weathered the storms of recent market turbulence and pandemics growing both the top and bottom lines through the dedication of the entire XLN team. I am proud to be associated with them.

Christian Nellemann is an admirable example of a man consumed by the accomplishment of his strategic goal of the ongoing success of XLN. Through his personal drive and total support for all colleagues, at all levels, in the organisation, XLN has grown in value and quality, as have employees of the company. During this period of impressive growth, he has remained a strong family man, achieving a solid work/family/pastime balance, and as such, one can but admire his approach to life. I count him as a dear friend and associate."

Frank McKay, Chairman of XLN

"Christian is an exceptional entrepreneur and a great business partner. We were constantly impressed by XLN's ability to quickly adapt to changing market dynamics and creatively solve challenges. We had an excellent relationship throughout our investment."

Michael Carruthers, Senior Managing Director, Blackstone Credit

"In my experience, it is very rare for a CEO to start a business from scratch and still be running it when it is the size that XLN is now. Managing and growing a business from start up through the ups and downs of economic cycles and four changes of investor to create XLN as it is today is an impressive accomplishment and we are proud to have been involved in part of the journey."

Tony Dickin, Partner at Palatine Private Equity LLP

RAW
BUSINESS

Every owner of a physical copy of this edition of

can download the eBook for free direct from us at
Harriman House, in a DRM-free format that can be read
on any eReader, tablet or smartphone.

Simply head to:

ebooks.harriman-house.com/rawbusiness

to get your copy now.

RAW

BUSINESS

A STRAIGHT-TALKING ACCOUNT OF WHAT IT MEANS TO BE A *SUCCESSFUL ENTREPRENEUR*

CHRISTIAN NELLEMANN

Harriman House

HARRIMAN HOUSE LTD
3 Viceroy Court
Bedford Road
Petersfield
Hampshire
GU32 3LJ
GREAT BRITAIN
Tel: +44 (0)1730 233870

Email: enquiries@harriman-house.com
Website: harriman.house

First published in Great Britain in 2021.
Copyright © Christian Nellemann

The right of Christian Nellemann to be identified as the Author has been asserted in accordance with the Copyright, Design and Patents Act 1988.

Paperback ISBN: 978-0-85719-890-7
eBook ISBN: 978-0-85719- 891-4

British Library Cataloguing in Publication Data
A CIP catalogue record for this book can be obtained from the British Library.

Whilst every effort has been made to ensure that information in this book is accurate, no liability can be accepted for any loss incurred in any way whatsoever by any person relying solely on the information contained herein.

No responsibility for loss occasioned to any person or corporate body acting or refraining to act as a result of reading material in this book can be accepted by the Publisher, by the Author, or by the employers of the Author.

A smart man learns from his mistakes, but a truly wise man learns from the mistakes of others.

Ken Schramm

*To all the amazing people that have helped me
and influenced me along the way. For all your
advice and love I am eternally grateful. Especially
my dad, K. E. K. Nellemann and my wonderful
wife Naima. Without your unwavering support I
couldn't have made it and without you in my life
it wouldn't have made any difference.
A huge thank you to the UK in general for taking
me in and allowing me to flourish.*

When you stop growing you start dying.

William S Burroughs

Contents

Introduction

MY WIFE, MY son Milo and I were having breakfast on the terrace of the Royal Riviera Hotel in Saint-Jean-Cap-Ferrat towards the end of August in 2019.

My mobile started vibrating and I picked it up. It was Alex Balkin, from Savills, my friend and real-estate broker in the South of France. He was chirpy and explained that the trustees had agreed to accept my offer for the villa of a well-known former head of state.

At 3pm we were sitting in the BA lounge awaiting our boarding call for our flight back to Britain when the phone rang again. Alex soberly explained that we had been gazumped by a real-estate developer who was able to complete quicker and with a higher deposit than us.

Ten minutes later my CEO, Neil Conaghan, called and explained that Equistone Private Equity had changed the goal posts yet again on the buy-out deal we had agreed.

I pulled the sale process. The deal was dead and my plans for the future, including a house in the South of France, were ruined. It was back to the grindstone and the drawing board to figure out what to do next.

But that's life and that's business.

It is said that everyone has a book in them, and I guess this is mine.

This book contains raw and unvarnished advice.

Its pages recount the story of my life and the lessons I've learnt along the way, as well as all the brilliant advice I've been fortunate enough to receive over the last half century.

It's a book on beating the odds, staying afloat where so many sink and growing where so many shrink. Based on my own real-life experiences – which span more than 30 years of running anything from home-based, to small and now multi-million-pound businesses – it's my tried and trusted model for achieving success.

Through the highs and lows, the good times and the bad, I have learnt what it takes to run a successful company and will share with you my formula for setting up, growing and managing both companies and people.

In the first part, I will recount my life story, from my childhood all the way through to starting XLN, and the life lessons I learnt along the way. Part two will outline the core principles I use to run my life and business – the principles that have been fundamental to my success. And finally, part three will pull these life lessons and core principles together, to show you how to start a successful business or grow your existing business into something far greater.

Very little in this book is original content; the mistakes are mine and the successes are largely due to all the great people I have worked with. The sage advice comes from people smarter and more successful than me.

It is my sincere hope that someone reading the following pages will take away a nugget or two of advice that will help them on their journey in business and life.

About Me

MY NAME IS Christian and I am what people call a 'serial entrepreneur'. I suppose that means I didn't really succeed the first time…

Selling products and starting businesses is like an addiction for me. I've been fascinated by the idea of business ever since I was a child and in the past 35 years have sold everything from wine, confectionery and perfumes to office products, telecoms and business utilities.

I'm proud to be a two-time winner of Ernst & Young's Entrepreneur of the Year award, to be one of only 14 people from the UK to be inducted into the Entrepreneur of the Year Global Hall of Fame, and to have been voted National CEO of the Year by the BVCA (British Venture Capital and Private Equity Association).

I'm passionate about small businesses and start-ups, and helping to build thriving, independent high streets across the UK.

With XLN, I have somehow managed to create a hugely successful business with over 110,000 customers and more than 450 staff. XLN makes £21m of EBITDA (profit before interest, tax, depreciation and amortisation) and is worth around £250m.

For an immigrant Danish boy who arrived in London at the age of 22 with little but an absolute determination to work hard and succeed, that feels pretty unreal. To be honest, this level of success was never in my wildest dreams – and I had big dreams.

I am not perfect by any means. I can be hot-headed and impatient, I find it hard to switch off, and I definitely shout too much when I'm excited about something.

But I am doing something that I love and somehow this incredible business has emerged as a result. XLN not only helps small businesses save money on essentials such as fibre broadband, Wi-Fi, credit-card processing and energy, it also champions and supports them every step of the way, so that they too can thrive and grow.

I thought it might be interesting to explain how I did it. I also wanted to help others by sharing the advice I was given and all the things I have learned the hard way that I wish I had known all those years ago.

PART
ONE

A Life Of
Lessons Learned

Chapter 1
Childhood

I HAVE HAD VERY mixed feelings about writing and publishing this book. In fact, I've been sitting on the final draft for the best part of a year and a half. On the one hand, I felt that passing on the lessons I've learnt and the scars I've accumulated throughout a 30-year career would potentially benefit someone. But on the other hand, I was self-consciously fearful that people would find it pretentious or would find the content dreadful.

Yet I am almost always asked what the fundamentals of running a successful business are? Can my success be replicated? What are the magic ingredients of success? What's the hidden formula? The secret sauce?

As a result, I've spent a fair amount of time thinking and talking about this, and I realised that my views are often different and, strangely enough, counterintuitive. A fair amount of advice you will have heard before, so I wanted to share my own unique experience of the business world too, in the hope that I can point hungry, ambitious entrepreneurs in the right direction.

If I can inspire just one entrepreneur to become successful or help someone avoid the ever-looming pitfalls that I fell victim to, then this foray into authorship will have been worthwhile.

There are a couple of reasons for writing this book. First, looking back over a career of building multi-million-pound businesses, I realised that my story was interesting because it gives a real insight into one of the most vital yet overlooked aspects of any successful business: how to build a fantastic sales team. Managing a sales operation well is fundamental to the success of any business, no matter what area it operates in, and yet many entrepreneurs have no idea how to create a sales team that really delivers.

Building an effective sales team is not difficult, but it does take hard work. Surprisingly, it is often left as an afterthought, something that is built on a foundation of little more than hope – hope that it's somehow going to just happen, that a team will just come together, and everything will fall into place. And that's where the problems start.

I have spent the last 30 years nurturing and training good salespeople, in order to create brilliant sales teams and hence successful companies. I wanted to share the knowledge I have learnt so that others can benefit from the very expensive 'school fees' I've had to pay along the way.

Another reason for putting pen to paper is that I would like to discuss the important role that culture plays within business. I am hoping that new employees of XLN will have a better understanding of why we do things the way we do and why XLN is such a different place to work.

Finally, I have two very young sons who have little to no interest in what Daddy does at work at the moment. If nothing else, I wanted there to be some sound fatherly advice to help them navigate life in case I'm not here when they need it.

This is primarily a business book, but rather than jump straight to my tips and advice without any perspective, I will start by telling the story of my journey as an entrepreneur right back from childhood. I think it's important to put things in context and provide a backdrop illustrating where my ideas were born, my advice was fashioned, and my core principles were developed.

I realise that everything I have learned in my life has emerged from influences I was exposed to while growing up and in particular, the wisdom and understanding that I gained from my father. I have been very fortunate to have had great mentors all throughout my life and career, and I owe it to all these people to pass their wisdom on.

We are, after all, the sum of our friends, family, and past experiences.

Right back at the beginning

My story begins in Denmark, in a small town called Kolding, not far from the German border. Kolding has a population of 60,000 people and is about the seventh largest town in Denmark, which is not saying much. Several industrial companies are based there but it is perhaps most noteworthy for its thirteenth-century castle, which is now home to the municipal museum of modern art, called the Koldinghus Museum.

It was the kind of place where even if you were successful, you didn't flaunt your wealth. Rich farmers and business people would drive old, inconspicuous cars so they didn't stand out, and their expensive watches would be hidden up their sleeve. Most had their feet firmly planted in the fertile soil – it reminds me most of the Yorkshire mentality.

My arrival into the world came as something of a surprise because my mother had been told that she could not have children. My birth also caused a bit of drama. I was born yellow, and the doctors thought I had serious, life-threatening levels of jaundice. I was immediately baptised and rushed in an ambulance, during a snowstorm, to another larger city's hospital, where I was in an incubator for a while. But I made it and came home.

Right from the start I was an adventurous child. I was always full of energy and was just 'go go go' all the time. I would be up at 5am and wouldn't stop moving until I went to bed. I was always up to all sorts of tricks. The first word I could say was 'hoover', and from an early age I would get the hoover out and start cleaning. And then I would get all the pots and pans out of the kitchen cupboards, much to my mother's annoyance.

At the age of three, I would unscrew light sockets. And as I grew older, I would run wild with my younger brother Peter and our friends. We were fearless, always making dens and swinging in trees over the road when cars were driving by. I must have been a bit of a nightmare for my parents. It got to the point where, if my mum was going over to see a friend, her friends would say, "you don't have to bring Christian".

My father owned a department store in town called Lumbye Inspiration and a timber business called Lumbye Industry. This afforded my family a comfortable lifestyle with a big house right on the fjord where we could swim and sail boats. My parents were very close friends with about six other families who lived close by and we spent a lot of time together. Every Friday and Saturday evening our house would be full of people drinking cocktails and eating little cocktail sausages – all the rage in the mid- to late-seventies – while the children ran around and played. The six families had holiday homes in the same place too, on an island called Fanoe, where we would all decamp during the summer months of June and July.

My father's business was very much part of our lives and as my younger brother Peter and I grew up, we would rarely see him at home because he was always working. He never came to events, such as our school sports day, so at the weekends, holidays and after school, I would go into the department store or the timber yard and hang around with my dad while he worked.

He could sometimes be strict though and we were quite frightened of him. Whenever I asked him whether I could come into work with him he would say yes, but if I wasn't ready on time, he would drive off without me. I remember very clearly to this day one morning where we had eaten breakfast together and I had asked to come with him to work. My dad would always leave the breakfast table, visit the bathroom and then leave. I mistimed his bathroom break and as I walked outside to the garage to get into the car with him, I saw his car already far down the road. That taught me an incredibly valuable lesson: be on time!

My dad taught me how to grow up fast. There's no doubt that he built my character with his focus on punctuality, commitment and drive. He always drummed into me that if you are going to do something, then you do it well and do it well the first time round.

Motivation

From a very early age I knew that I wanted to be a businessman too, like my father, and his father before him. Either that or a gangster, as I apparently told my somewhat concerned mum at the tender age of six. One thing was clear; I wanted to be successful, and I wanted to be rich.

I wanted to have all the nice things in life, like cars, boats and houses, and I wanted a lot of wonderful experiences, such as travel and great food, all of which required a huge amount of money.

I also understood very early on that money buys freedom. My dad always told me that when you make your own money, you can make your own decisions. So I was always thinking about how I could start making some money of my own.

My grandmother, whom I absolutely adored, lived in a large apartment above my father's department store, so I would often go and visit her when I went into work with him. She had a large key that could open all the doors in the business, so I would sometimes take it and wander around the building after it had closed for customers. I particularly loved rummaging around in the inventory room where there were all kinds of interesting things.

When I was about seven years old, I found some eggs made out of plaster in the inventory room. Farmers would buy them to put into chicken nests because the presence of an egg encourages the chicken to lay more. I bought some of these eggs with my pocket money and decided to dip them in yellow and purple gloss paint with a sprinkling of gold and silver glitter on top. I attached a little gold or silver thread to each one and sold them to neighbours at Easter. I ended up making and selling dozens of them.

Even at that age, I was already showing an entrepreneurial spirit and putting some of my dad's wisdom into practice. Even though I, at the time, resented the repetitive nature of my dad's advice, I'm forever grateful to him for that.

LIFE LESSON

You have to build it yourself, because no-one else is going to build it for you. No-one else is going to make you successful.

I learnt the hard way that it is always better to pay for the things I want.

My dad's department store also sold sports equipment, and up in the attic there were boxes of all sorts of stuff, including fishing tackle. I never really went fishing, but these fishing tackles looked really nice – a bit like jewellery, because they were made from shiny brass and brightly coloured enamel. I was fascinated by them. I used to take a couple of them every now and then, one from each box, so that no-one would notice they were missing. But one day I went too far; I went with my friends to another store in the town, one of my dad's smaller competitors, and stole some fishing tackle from there too.

The following night I was having dinner with my parents and brother when my dad suddenly looked at me. He told me to go up to my bedroom and bring down the white plastic bag that was at the top of my cupboard, behind my clothes.

It was the plastic bag with the fishing tackle in. I have no idea how he had found out about it, but I had to go and get the bag and admit that I had stolen the fishing tackle. The next day, the two of us drove into his workplace and then we walked hand in hand from his office down to the store of his competitor. The owner came out of a room at the back and said, "Mr Nellemann, what are you are doing here? What a surprise." My dad told him that sadly he had come with some really bad news and that his son had something he would like to say.

I was so embarrassed, both on my own and on my father's behalf. He would have been absolutely furious about any kind of stealing, but the fact that I had stolen from one of his competitors was just terrible. That he stood there mortified and took the shame with me made such an impression on me that I have never so much as stolen a lollipop ever since.

That said, I did continue to get into trouble. One winter when I was about ten, my father got a call from a neighbour while he was at work. My brother, a friend and I had been spotted jumping from ice slab to ice slab on the fjord by our house – it was almost frozen over, but not quite – and we were about half a mile out to sea.

My dad dropped everything and rushed down to his car. It must have been the most terrifying journey of his life. Fortunately, by the time he reached the edge of the fjord we had already come in. He smacked my brother and me hard on the bottom and we were sent to our rooms. It was the only time he ever smacked us. And it was the only time we ever went out onto the ice slabs. We had learnt our lesson.

Big events have real impact, a notion I have carried through into my business career. You must learn and move on.

School days

I went to the local school until I was 11, but during the summer holidays my family visited some friends. One of their sons, Christian, was at boarding school and the other, Ditlev, was about to join him. It sounded really exciting, so I asked my parents if I could go too. In those days, it was extremely unusual to send children to boarding school in Denmark, and it still is now. But I saw it as an opportunity to spread my wings. I had never really liked the confined space of a small town where everybody knows you. For me, it just meant that if I did something wrong, my father would be told and he would be disappointed. I didn't particularly like being well known because of my dad's businesses either. I liked the idea of anonymity.

My mother was really upset at the idea of me going away and cried for days, but my father could see how much I wanted to go. He agreed to send me to boarding school on the condition that I stay there for at least one year. He told me that I couldn't just decide that I wanted to leave after three months if I didn't like it.

I agreed, and so a few months later my parents drove me to Herlufsholm School, a highly-respected school for boys about 50 miles south-west of Copenhagen.

Joining the school was a big shock, however. The school was originally founded in 1565 to educate the nobility, and many high-ranking families still sent their sons there. I found myself in the same class as the sons of earls and barons, rich kids from Copenhagen and famous people's kids. I was used to being the leader of my little group of friends back at home but now I found that I was pretty much at the bottom of the pecking order.

To make matters worse, I was a slightly chubby kid because I had broken my leg that summer and couldn't play football or any other sports. It didn't help that I had started in school a year early and some of the boys in my class had stayed back a year, so I was younger than almost everyone else. I was also one of the shortest boys in the year and remained so until I was about 14 years old. When you are a child, that kind of thing makes an enormous difference.

All of this caused problems for me; I didn't like feeling inferior and fought against it. I couldn't accept my place in the new pecking order and initially it was really difficult.

Even though it had been my choice to come, I was really homesick and for the first few months I cried myself to sleep most nights. I would call home in tears. But at the end of the first year, I decided to stay and tough it out. I didn't want to be someone who quit.

As time went by, I did make some friends, but I was never one of the popular crowd and was in fact really unpopular at times. I developed some very effective defence mechanisms to protect myself and could be pretty sharp tongued if someone put me down.

Fortunately, I only ever got into one fight.

The school had a rather odd tradition – if you wanted to fight with somebody you would challenge them to a fist fight and then the news would spread amongst the boys during dinner. There was a river running through the school grounds and nearby there was a little island with a moat around it, which probably hadn't been cleaned for 200 years.

There was a small wooden bridge across to the island and when there was a fight taking place all the boys would stand around this island and watch. The two opponents would walk across to the island and fight until one of them gave up. The winner would then walk back over the bridge and the loser would have to jump over the moat. I only ever witnessed one boy manage that feat. The rest would sink up to their neck in the foul-smelling silt.

Luckily, I won.

LIFE LESSON

You have to face up to changes, challenges and challengers.

Making money

As time went on, I began to find ways of making money by being a bit entrepreneurial. Lessons finished at 2pm every afternoon and we had free time until study time at 4:15pm. During my first year there, when I was 11, I got a job in an antiquarian bookseller in the local town. I would mind the shop for a couple of hours two afternoons a week while the owner took a break. I was paid the equivalent of £1 an hour, which substantially topped up the £1.50 pocket money I received each week.

One day, I found a case of porn magazines under one of the shelves and asked the owner of the shop if I could borrow them. I brought them back to school and rented them out to my classmates for the equivalent of 2.5p for half an hour at a time. It was a bit like pay-per-view TV. We would sit and look at the magazines in one of the common rooms. I got caught, of course. My housemaster dragged me out of bed one evening and pulled me down the stairs by my hair and then slapped me around. I got pretty beaten up, but it was worth it.

Then, a couple of years later – when I was 14 – I hit upon another money-making idea. The only way of getting sweets at school was to either buy them from a shop in the town or from the petrol station, a 20-minute walk away. I came up with a better plan.

One of my dad's friends, Arnd Lentz, was on the board of Rowntree, the confectionery firm, in Denmark. They made Lion Bars, English wine gums and Super Flyers, a kind of liquorice sweet that we loved. There was a telephone in one of the common rooms, so I called Rowntree and got through to their sales department. I managed to get them to open an account for me – obviously with a bit of help from my dad's friend.

Every few weeks I would call them up and place an order for a couple of cases of Super Flyers, wine gums and Lion Bars and get them delivered to me at school. Then I would hide the sweets in the cupboard in my study and sell them to my classmates. It was great business. Unfortunately, the headmaster's wife found out I was selling sweets to all my classmates. She was a dentist and didn't think it was a good idea, and so my highly successful business got shut down.

As I grew older, I calmed down a bit and eventually became friends with one of the most popular boys in the school, Henrik. We are still best mates to this day. That settled some of my inferiority complex. But such insecurities never really go away; I still have a bit of an inferiority complex now, despite my success, and that goes right back to being at that school.

However, these experiences also taught me to never give up. I never quit something that I have started, regardless of how tough the going may be. Whenever I get knocked back, I just get back up and carry on. It's an important trait to have. To succeed you must be persistent, tough, passionate and relentless.

As my old boss in America used to say, "winners never quit and quitters never win". So true.

LIFE LESSON

Attitude is everything. Never quit. Never ever give up. Learn to be resilient and relentless.

Chapter 2
Starting Out In Business

With your hands or your head?

WHEN I LEFT boarding school at the age of 18, many of my friends went interrailing around Europe. I wanted to go with them, but my dad refused, saying that I'd basically already had one long holiday by being at boarding school.

And when my dad said no, it was no. That was the end of it.

Instead, he arranged for me to spend a year learning English at a language school in Cambridge. And because the course didn't start until September, he found me a job working in a warehouse in the north of Denmark over the summer.

Every day, 17-tonne articulated trucks would arrive from Poland stacked with cases of porcelain cups, saucers and plates. I had to unload them all onto palettes, shrink-wrap each palette and then take them away on a trolley. It was laborious, tiring, and mind-numbingly boring. I had to get up at 5:30am each morning to start work at 7am and we would finish at 4pm. After working for three months, my dad said, "now you know what it is like working with your hands so you can now decide whether you want to work with your head or your hands in life". I thought, actually, I want to work with my head.

After a year in Cambridge, I had hoped to join the two-year officers training programme for the Queens Guard regiment, the bearskin guards who protect the Queen of Denmark. I applied along with several of my classmates. Boys from my school would typically go into either the Queens Guard or the Hussars, which were the two most prestigious regiments in Denmark, and I wanted to as well.

Disappointingly, I was told that there was a two-year waiting list and I was too impatient to wait that long. Patience is not my strong point. I wanted to start making money. So I went back to Denmark and took a Bachelor of Science degree in economics and business analysis at the University of Southern Denmark, which was in my hometown. I went back to live at home, but my parents were mostly away travelling so I was on my own most of the time.

Like my friends, I would often kill time between lessons by sailing on the fjord. And although it is beautiful out there, I quickly realised that I needed something else to occupy my spare time.

I decided to try and make a bit of money selling wine by mail order. One of my dad's friends had a business which imported wine from Portugal, so I got in touch and arranged to buy cases of wine from him at a wholesale rate and sell it on. I liked wine, having always been surrounded by it at home. The wine he was selling was cheap – at the equivalent of just £2 a bottle – so I thought I would be able to sell some. At that time, mail order was very popular, so I bought some books on the subject and a mailing list of potential customers, and starting creating enticing mail-order letters to send out; lots of highlighting, lots of red and blue pen.

It was a straightforward operation to run – whenever I got an order, I would arrange for the wine to be sent out directly from the warehouse where my dad's friend stored the wine. That meant I didn't have to buy or store any stock myself. The business wasn't very successful though because I didn't get enough orders, and the profit margins were too small to make it worthwhile.

━━━━ **LIFE LESSON** ━━━━

When you fail, you learn. It doesn't matter if you invest your efforts in something that doesn't work out, as long as you learn from it and move on. I call it school fees. People that stand still never fail, never learn, and never win. Don't be afraid of failure.

———————

After that, I tried selling men's shirts by mail order, also imported from Portugal, but that wasn't a great success either. Again, because I didn't get enough orders. The mail-order business wasn't as easy as it looked.

However, both of these ventures did teach me some valuable lessons about business. The key to success is to control the distribution channel for your product or service, and to control the relationship with the customer. I didn't need to own the wine or the warehouse, because I could find people who already did that, and holding stock can be an expensive nightmare. But if you are in charge of product distribution and the relationship with the customer, then you are king.

I had made a plan for when I finished my BSc at university. I wanted to do an MBA at Harvard Business School and go on to learn barter trading in Austria for a year. Then I wanted to go to Taiwan to build relationships with businesses there, before beginning to trade with China. I would have had to wait for that last goal though, as in those days China hadn't opened up to the outside world. With a bit of luck, I would probably have been really successful by now if I had done that. In hindsight, that wasn't a bad plan at all. But life is easy in hindsight.

The sweet smell of early success

But life intervened, as it so often does, and another opportunity presented itself. In 1988, in the summer holiday between my second and third year of university, another of my dad's friends sent us some bottles of perfume. They were copies of famous perfumes – Opium, Obsession, Giorgio, Poison, Oscar de la Renta, etc. – made in the same factories in Grasse, in the south of France, as the original versions.

My dad's friend, who was the general consul for Denmark in Hawaii, had noticed them because his son was involved with the company selling them; he thought they might be something that my dad would be interested in. In reality, I think he was looking for a commission and after I started in Mile End, his son came knocking.

The perfumes all smelled the same as the original fragrances, but they were called another name and came in different colour-coded packaging. They were entirely legitimate too, because there is nothing illegal about copying a smell. I was fascinated by them, and I was particularly fascinated by the fact that the owner of the business had made $100m selling these perfumes door to door.

So my dad flew down to meet the American owner, Larry Hahn, while he was holidaying in Monaco and managed to acquire the rights to import and sell the perfumes in most of Europe. Unfortunately, this did not include the UK. Then, in December 1988, I flew over to San Francisco with my dad to see the sales operation there and learn more about the whole set-up. I was supposed to spend six months writing two dissertations for my degree, but I wrote them really quickly so I could go out to San Francisco for two months instead.

When I arrived in the big US of A it was pretty daunting to be honest. I was a young boy from a very small town and America was just so big – San Francisco was amazing though. It was actually quite European, and I instantly felt at home. I wasn't homesick either, years at boarding school had long since cured that affliction.

I arrived on Saturday. The following day, Sunday, Kerry Brunson, the regional-sales office owner I had been assigned to train with, took me and his entire sales office to Golden Gate Park, where we played American football, had a barbeque, drank beer and had lots of fun together.

In those days, and in the many years to follow, I always mixed business with pleasure and I still believe that having a fun time outside of the office together with your team is a good thing to do. Sadly, nowadays that is pretty much a no-no, as fraternising with employees comes with an increasing dose of danger. I find that very sad and certainly not in the best interest of the business or the employees. I strongly believe that a business is made better by employees seeing a more human side of the boss outside of work.

However, always bear in mind that even if you are relaxing and hanging out with employees, you are still at work. You will find that staff will ask you all sorts of questions in the mistaken belief that because you are not in the office, you are going to tell them a different story to what you'd otherwise say. You should never do that. For some reason, people think that just because you are having a beer together in a pub or at some company jolly, that you are now going to tell them the real truth. Always be on your guard but use these occasions to get closer to your team.

On Monday, we were back in the office at 7am. Every day started the same way, with a managers meeting from 7:30 to 8am. Then all the sales guys would arrive and get 'settled up', which meant they would get their perfumes for the day ahead and pay for any sales taken overnight or during the weekend. We always worked Saturdays and some guys that needed to hit their weekly target worked on Sundays too. The American work ethic hit me like a steam train.

Once the administrative side of the business had been taken care of, we all assembled for a morning meeting. This started with a roll call of evening or weekend production, and then a tally of total sales per person for the week just passed. These numbers would be written up on a whiteboard at the front of the meeting room.

We would then have a 'pitch class', where a manager would act as a prospective customer and a selection of sales guys would take it in turns to pitch to them in front of the entire office. That could be a bit daunting for a new recruit, but it did help toughen you up and I learned that constant repetition was key to teaching salespeople good work habits. By repeating good sales practices every morning for 15 minutes, each pitch being 3–4 minutes, eventually these habits would sink in and take over when you were in the field. I have continued to advocate pitch classes ever since. It really does work, even though it might seem a bit childish.

After the meeting I was paired up with my two trainers for the day. We travelled in their car to a little town called Walnut Creek, which lay across the Oakland Bay Bridge in an area that is now very gentrified – many from Silicon Valley choose to live there. Back then, it was a real dump.

For the morning stint I worked with Eldon Schwartz, who used to be a TV presenter for a local station, and he was an amazing salesman. We worked a local strip of small businesses and walked into hairdressers and small shops. Eldon, who was in his fifties, had a great pitch which I later copied. He would walk through the door to, for example, a hair salon full of women and say: "Hi, I'm the male stripper you ordered". Then he would stay silent and wait for the penny to drop.

This inevitably resulted in a laugh – the ice would be broken and Eldon would have their undivided attention. He would then launch into his pitch that he had some great perfumes that smelled the same as popular fragrances – we called them renditions rather than knock-offs – and cost a quarter of the real thing. Eldon sold 34 bottles that morning. I was flabbergasted. It looked easy and was so much fun.

For the afternoon session I was paired up with a young guy called Mike Tessier, who'd later go on to open the first sales office in Australia. He sold 22 bottles that Monday afternoon. In the space of a day, I saw them sell 56 bottles of perfume combined. I was sold and convinced that this job would be a doddle. How wrong I was.

My first week I sold a total of three bottles – the last two of which, made on the Friday, were more of a sympathy sale than anything else. I was hopeless at selling. My second week, I sold 21 bottles. On my third week, I participated in a road trip. This was when four salespeople got in a car loaded up with merchandise and travelled to an area that was seldom hit. I sold a total of 31 bottles that week.

The idea that travelling to a new territory will make sales easier is, of course, partially a myth. But for a salesperson, the key is that you are away from all the distractions of home. You can focus more and, importantly, you can work longer hours. Road trips were a big part of training new agents back in those days. It was thought to be a great way of getting a new recruit properly engaged and 'brainwashed'.

Once back from the road trip, I had another feeble week of 24 sales. Not good at all, considering a decent sales guy would sell around 40–50 bottles a week; a good one, 60–70; and the truly great could sell 100 in a day but would breeze easily into the 100-club each week.

But I learned a lot of valuable lessons about discipline, work habits, attitude and enthusiasm. This whole new concept of attitude and enthusiasm was fascinating to me. And God did I get a baptism of fire in hard work and solid work habits. I had never seen anything like it before and I felt that I worked like a dog. Could one really work any harder? I thought not.

A life-changing moment

On the back of four weeks of pretty mediocre sales performance, I unexpectedly received a phone call from Kerry Brunson's boss, Billy Reynolds. Billy had started the sales organisation I now belonged to. Back in the 70s, it was called The Dazzlers and encompassed 200 sales offices across the US.

Kerry's organisation was called The Sunshine Dazzlers and one day my organisation would be known as The Glooden Boogen Dazzlers, because Kerry always joked that when I spoke Danish on the phone with my parents it sounded like glooden boogen jigen jagen. I digress. Kerry found me working in the sales meeting room and told me there was a call for me from the vice president, who was calling from the head office in Atlanta, Georgia.

I was pretty excited about speaking to the legend Billy Reynolds, but that excitement soon evaporated and was replaced by utter doom and gloom. In not so many words, Billy said something along the lines of, "Christian, I've followed your early sales progress and it is pure bull****. Clearly you are a weak piece of crap so why don't you go back to Denmark because you are never going to amount to anything".

In those days, we had a weekly newsletter that recorded individual and office sales-production standings across the entire US organisation of 15,000 salespeople. In my state of shock and utter shame, I exclaimed, "Mr Reynold, I'm not a useless piece of crap and I'll prove it to you. Next week, I'm going to do a 100-club". A 100-club was the highest sales achievement an agent could attain, and mythical stories abound of agents hitting the fabled 100 sales within a week. Of course, I had very little chance of hitting this lofty target and certainly not after a week selling just 24 bottles – my best week so far had been 31 sales. But the gauntlet had been thrown, so I set about figuring out how I was going to make the impossible happen.

Numbers and economics had always been my thing, so I started to figure out how I could possibly hit 100 sales in one week. I started with my current best sales performance of 5–6 sales per day, or 31 for a five-day week. Five sales per day had been achieved by me working from around 11am to 5pm, with the time from 9am and after 5pm spent travelling to and from my territory.

I figured that if I started working at 9am and worked until midnight, I could increase my working hours by a factor of 2.5, which should yield around 15 sales. If I then worked all seven days of the week, Monday through to Sunday night, I could theoretically hit 100 sales. In order to build in some slack – in case I had a bad day – I decided that I had to plan to hit the 100 sales by Saturday night, meaning I needed 17 sales per day. A monumental task but theoretically possible based on longer hours and more days, as well as increased focus, intensity and enthusiasm.

I worked all the hours – often until way past midnight – and by Sunday night, at 1:30am, I hit 104 sales. Notice that I didn't just stop at 100 but kept working until I literally couldn't stand upright any longer.

The following morning I asked Kerry if I could borrow the office phone and have Billy Reynolds' number in Atlanta. I called the head office and was eventually put through to Billy who took my call. "Mr Reynolds", I said triumphantly, "this is Christian Nellemann and I did my 100-club last week, so **** you" and hung up.

This might have been one of the most important lessons of my early career. This experience taught me what hard work really is all about. Most importantly, I taught myself that when you really put your mind and your backside to something, it is unbelievable what you can achieve.

I quadrupled my sales performance from one week to the next simply on the back of increased focus, planning and determination, as well as working bloody hard and insanely long hours. This lesson formed my early career and has stayed with me ever since. I have no doubt that it has been a major contributor to my success in life.

LIFE LESSON

Get out of bed early and get mentally prepared for the day ahead. You must develop a positive mindset and then work incredibly hard in an organised and disciplined manner on your daily goal.

The Glooden Boogen Dazzlers

The idea had been that I was going to set up a company and a sales operation for our new perfume venture in Hamburg, Germany, so I translated all the training and operational material into German. Fortunately, I already spoke German because as a child I had grown up watching German television. When I was young, there was only one Danish television station, which started broadcasting at 6pm each evening, but because we lived close to the German border, we were also able to watch the three German channels which broadcast throughout the day. I was pretty proficient in German by the time I was 12 years old.

My dad and I registered trademarks for the business and found offices in Hamburg, as well as shippers and lawyers. But then, about two weeks before I finished studying and planned to move to Hamburg, the American owner of the business began to pull the 'fear of loss' card and told my dad that he needed to place an order immediately for 10,000 bottles of perfume in order to keep the rights to the countries we had agreed on.

My dad refused, saying that we needed to sort out several issues before we could commit to buying such a large amount of stock. But the owner was insistent, saying that we had to buy the stock because he had other people queueing up to take the sales rights for Germany. So my dad walked away from the deal. Obviously there were no other interested parties, but it was a classic American hustle. Unfortunately, my dad doesn't respond well to that kind of salesmanship and he told the American where to go.

My dad called me into his office one evening to tell me what had transpired and that our perfume venture was not going ahead. But this was my bright exciting future; it was a week before I graduated from business school and I was all set to move to Hamburg and start the business. My dad was adamant that he didn't want to do business with a *schuft* (spiv) like Larry Hahn, but I was likewise determined not to give up on my American Perfume Dream. So he agreed to give me a £100,000 advance on my inheritance and told me that I could go ahead without him, but that I was on my own. That gave me a real burning desire to succeed and filled me with equal measures of fear and excitement.

I called the owner in America and asked him what my options were. He told me that I could have the exclusive rights to sell the perfumes in Canada instead, starting in Toronto, and as I expanded I could eventually gain the exclusive rights to all of Canada. I said that was fine with me, as long as I could come to America again and learn from his best sales leaders first – I wanted as much time as I deemed necessary. He agreed.

Hence, a week after I graduated, I moved to San Francisco. I spent months travelling around the country to meet his top sales leaders and selling perfume on commission only. I knew that I had to experience the proper training programme but I also sensed that learning everything I could from his very best sales leaders would stand me in good stead down the road. So, after having spent three months training, I started visiting all the top sales offices and organisations across the country.

Then, one day, while back in San Francisco, Larry invited me out to lunch at a very snazzy Italian restaurant and told me that I could have the exclusive rights to the UK after all, if I would like them. I said I would love to set up in the UK, as it was so much closer to home than Canada. Within two weeks, I had packed up all my stuff, said goodbye to all my newfound American friends, and moved to London.

Last train to London

I stayed in a motel in Kings Cross while I looked for offices and eventually found one that I could just about afford in Mile End in the East End of London. I sorted out lawyers, shippers and accountants, and figured out where I would advertise to recruit salespeople.

I had happened upon Mile End while travelling on the Central Line, which I'd been told was the more reliable Tube line. Office space towards the West End was very expensive in those days and it was only once in Mile End that I found anything even remotely within my budget. Across the street from the Mile End tube station was a road called Aberavon Road and I was told by the local estate agent that a pair of property developers, John Baker and Nick Barrington Peace, had an office to let. So I knocked on their door and was shown the building next door, which was in the middle of being renovated. We agreed a deal for me to rent the building. I then went back to Denmark to get all my things ready for my permanent move to the UK. That was in late 1989; I was 22 years old.

The office I thought I had done a deal to rent included accommodation above it, but when I turned up to move in, the property wasn't ready. Understandably, John Baker had assumed that I would never turn up again. I didn't want to spend any more money on motels, so for the first three nights I slept on the carpet in the reception area of my new landlord's office with only a towel over me.

When the property was finally ready to move into, I started making a few changes. I turned the dingy room on the lower ground floor into a sales meeting room and kitted it out with some whiteboards; the adjoining bathroom became the merchandise room and the reception room at the front upstairs was turned into an interview room where I could recruit new salespeople. There was a little conservatory at the back, which was my office, and on the first floor there was a bedroom for Sharon, a sales manager from San Francisco, who I had recruited to help me start up and run the business. The attic was my bedroom.

We started selling the perfumes in exactly the same way as I had been trained to sell them in San Francisco, by taking them door to door into businesses and selling them to the employees.

Sharon Kelley was a huge support and help in starting the business; without her help, I'm sure I wouldn't have succeeded. Sharon stayed with me for four years until her visa finally ran out and she sadly returned to the States. I often wonder what has become of her and hope she has become as successful and happy as she rightly deserved to be.

I had agreed with the American owner that I would buy the perfumes from him at a wholesale rate but that I would decide everything else about how the business was run, including how much to sell the perfumes for. This meant I was buying the bottles at $3.50 each and selling them for £15, and later for £20 when the VAT rate went up from 17.5% to 20%. I basically wanted to be in exactly the same position as the American owner.

I called the business Scentura Creations Ltd., the same name as the business in the US, and started to build a sales team. I recruited people who were prepared to come in and work hard and learn how to sell. It was commission only and a very tough gig.

Once my salespeople had learnt how to sell, I would teach them how to train somebody else to do the same thing. When they were able to train somebody else, I would teach them how to manage a team of salespeople. And when they could do that, I would open a new sales office for them. I would pay for the furniture and give them money to start up, and they would then start recruiting people and training them exactly how I had shown them. If they worked hard, they could make a lot of money and have their own business.

I soon developed my own method of teaching people how to sell. It wasn't a particularly English approach to selling, but it wasn't a very Danish approach either. Instead, it was more of an American way of doing things, combined with a philosophy of continuous incremental improvement which meant that I was constantly looking for ways in which we could do better.

The business began to do really well. At £20 for 100ml of eau de parfum, our perfumes cost a fraction of the price of the real perfumes, which could sell for up to £80 for 100ml, and yet most people could not tell the difference.

On the box

We even managed to get the perfumes on the ITV breakfast show *This Morning*, with Richard Madeley and Judy Finnigan. One of my office owners, Jonathan Fitchew, later of Pareto Law fame, went onto the show with several of our perfumes and Richard and Judy sprayed a different one on the hand of four models. Then they sprayed the real versions of the perfumes on the models' other hand. Then they smelt each of them in turn to see if they could work out which was the real perfume and which was our fake version. Each time they thought that our perfumes were the real thing – and they even preferred three of our perfumes to the genuine versions. It became a lot easier to sell our perfumes after that because suddenly everyone wanted them.

Even though I was effectively starting a business in a foreign country, I never found it a problem being Danish because I think that the Danes and the Brits have more in common than what sets us apart, particularly our sense of humour. If anything, the biggest barrier was my age. When I started recruiting people, I was only 22 years old and I looked younger. I literally looked like a young boy. But I approached it in the way that I approach all these things and made the barrier into a strength. I would say, look at me, I am 22 years old, I have never had a job, and yet I am the boss here and I'm doing really well, so it has got to be a pretty good system. Basically, if I can do it, you can do it.

As sales continued to grow, I opened up offices all over the UK until I had a team of 200 salespeople, all working on commission only. Then I opened offices in Denmark, Germany, Austria, Holland, Italy and Greece. The international offices were owned by other people and I just supplied them with perfume on a wholesale basis.

I was making a lot of money. Just four years after the business started, when I was 25, I was able to buy a large first-floor flat in Eaton Place, one of the most prestigious addresses in London.

I even briefly thought about retiring, but after a week of doing nothing, I was so bored that I couldn't wait to get back to work and keep growing the business.

Everything slips

One New Year's Eve, my dad told me that I had made more money that year than all his businesses combined. He also told me that he was proud of me for the first time in my life.

And in that single moment, I lost all my motivation.

I virtually stopped working and I didn't pay enough attention to the business, because the driving force had always been to gain my dad's approval and recognition. Now I had received that recognition, my driving force had completely vanished. I stopped putting in the effort that the business needed and so it pretty much disintegrated. Over the following few years, the sales network shrank from 200 people to 12 people.

Meanwhile, I was partying hard. I was young and had earned a lot of money and I wanted to enjoy myself. I started taking the party drug ecstasy and when I got scared that it might be dangerous, I switched to taking cocaine because for some reason I thought it might be safer. Insane, I know. I also drank a lot of vodka. I would go out on a Saturday night with my brother and some friends, or with select people from work, and we would cram a huge amount into that one night. It was getting to the point where I began to realise that it might end badly.

Fortunately, I do perform well when I have my back against the wall. When I turned 30 in 1997, I realised that I was about to lose what little I had left and that I needed to make some big changes. So I stopped drinking, I stopped taking drugs, I stopped partying and I started exercising and eating properly. I pulled myself together, got into recovery and got serious.

I also decided that I didn't want to have any more handouts from my family and that I needed to stand on my own two feet. At the time, my mum and dad would often pay for things in my life because I had thrown most of my money away, but their generosity would sometimes come with strings attached. They would come around to my flat and offer to pay for some new curtains, for example, but then my mum would turn up with the fabrics she had chosen. I realised that constantly being funded like that could make for a very unhappy life and that I needed to forge my own path. I know they meant well though and only wanted to help their boy.

I started focusing on the business again and over the next two years I gradually built it back up, on the way developing an even better sales programme than before.

LIFE LESSON

Motivation is everything. If you need to understand one thing, it's the honest answer to the question: "What gets me out of bed every morning?" If you are not moving forwards, you will inevitably start to slip backwards. Don't ever take your eye off the ball.

During this time, the factors underlying the business had also started to change. Office space was becoming even more expensive and currency and shipping costs for the perfumes were rising, so the overheads of opening new sales offices had crept up. Yet we couldn't put the price of the perfume up because people would have stopped buying it. So there was no longer the potential of making large amounts of money that there used to be.

I was still promoting the business and telling new recruits to trust me, saying that if they did what I told them to do, they would be successful – provided they were willing to work really hard. The problem was that towards the end of the 90s, that wasn't true. You couldn't really make money running one of our sales offices like you used to be able to. I was still making great money myself, but I was peddling something that I didn't believe in anymore. Many other people would perhaps have carried on, but I realised that I was not prepared to sell 'the dream' if I knew full well that the end goal wasn't as rosy as I was claiming. So I shut the business down. I wanted to do the right thing by my team.

I ended up having a few thousand bottles of perfume left over, worth about £20,000, so I gave them to a friend in America, who was in the same business and in financial trouble, to help him out. Again, it felt like the right thing to do and frankly I had no use for the perfumes anymore.

LIFE LESSON

A business is only as trustworthy as the person behind it and the values it is built on. Be true to yourself and the people that rely on you. Don't do anything that will make it hard for you to look at yourself honestly in the mirror every morning.

In business, you have to be able to stand up and justify what you are doing and why. If you can't, then you should stop doing it. You are accountable for others and you have to do the right thing by them and by yourself.

It was a hard decision to contemplate but once I had made the decision to shut the perfume business down, I felt a huge weight lifted. And as they say, "when one door closes another opens". I'm not a quitter and this wasn't about giving up, but sometimes you naturally come to the end of the road. Everything has its time, as my dad would often say, and I had reached the end of this particular one. On to the next thing.

Chapter 3

From Perfume
To Office Products

WHILE I WAS still running the perfume business, I also got involved in an office-products business. Around Christmas 1993, my dad and I were introduced to David Whittaker, David Langdon and James Wilson. They had founded a mail-order office-supplies company together with a big PLC called Centurion Press and were now in financial trouble. Eventually, after long deliberation and negotiation, we bought a 51% stake in the business, called XPD. It had two major brands, OfficePoint and OfficeStar.

My brother came in the following year to help run the business and became the financial director. I was a non-executive director on the board.

The firm was really good at making mail-order catalogues and the original plan was to create a business similar to Viking Direct, which sold office supplies by mail order to companies. Viking Direct was super successful in those days and mailed around 30 million catalogues a year. However, when I started looking in closer detail at the business model, it became clear to me that the business was not going to ever become successful because it needed too much investment. In order to penetrate the market, XPD needed to send out a huge number of catalogues every week, but that required millions of pounds to do properly. We weren't prepared to put up that amount of capital, so we had to change the model.

Instead we refocused the business on its strengths and started making catalogues for other office-supplies dealers around the country, which they could then send out to their customers. When that went well, we began to send the catalogues out to customers ourselves, on their behalf. We also started to recruit more and more dealers to join our 'marketing group'.

And then we realised that we could also act on behalf of these office-supplies companies when it came to buying stock. We could negotiate with the wholesalers to get much lower prices because we were buying in bulk. We would receive a 'retro' from the wholesalers, a commission on the stock we were buying on behalf of the marketing group, and we would also take a fee for creating their catalogues and sending them out.

All of a sudden, we had a buying and marketing group of 400 office-supplies dealers which combined had a turnover of £250m. XPD's brands OfficePoint and OfficeStar became two of the three biggest office-supplies groups in the country. We also started creating other buying and marketing groups, including one called Computer Point and another called Cadpoint.

The internet calls

In early 1999, while I was in the process of closing down the perfume business, the internet began to happen in earnest. I thought that it seemed really interesting but more than that, I realised that it could offer something that no other market could – a level playing field. Here was a completely new industry, if you could call it that, where nobody knew more about it than me or anybody else.

I knew I had a good mindset, that I was industrious and willing to work harder than almost anybody else, so I realised that I could have a real advantage here. In any other market you get into, there is always a large incumbent company in place or other businesses who have been doing it for a long time before you, but not in this case. Best of all, unlike me, everyone else was already deeply invested in bricks and mortar type businesses – they couldn't change their direction as quickly as I could.

So I thought, this could be it.

I had an idea. I approached the owners of the businesses that were members of XPD's office-supplies group and suggested that we combine forces to create a national chain of businesses with a single common identity. At that time, every one of the 400 businesses had exactly the same set-up. They had a receptionist, an office, a warehouse, an employee in the warehouse, a delivery driver and a van, one or two salespeople on the phone or road, an accountant and so on. Yet these were all overheads, and meant that from the roughly £1m that each business might turn over, it would end up making just £25,000 profit.

I realised that the internet meant we could centralise a lot of these functions and take huge amounts of overheads out. By creating a national chain with a single brand identity, we could bring together all the individual accounting, telesales and customer-service functions into one central back-office team, and we could get all the orders delivered direct to customers from the wholesale suppliers.

This would mean that every single one of the 400 businesses in the group could get rid of their warehouse, their delivery driver, their van, their accountant, their receptionist and their customer-service staff. In other words, they could take out pretty much all their expensive overheads and 'outsource' it to our common entity. They could keep their salespeople and get them out on the road selling, thereby growing their business. Often an office-supplies dealer would start life as a salesman that had gone independent in the hope of building a successful business for themselves. However, the admin side of running a dealer was such that it usually got in the way of selling to customers and growing the company. Hence, very few dealers ever made it above £1m in turnover and most were around £500k per year.

I explained to these owners that doing this could also provide them with a way of getting some money out of their business which they couldn't access before, because they could sell the premises that they no longer needed. They could buy a villa in Marbella if they wanted to. We would then list the entire group company on the stock exchange and thereby create liquidity for the owners to eventually exit their life's work. This was often not an option and most of the time a dealer was difficult to sell at a half-decent price.

It was a brilliant plan. At least, I thought so.

The problem was I just couldn't get these office dealers to see it. They argued that their customers wanted their business to have a local identity. They thought that the fact their business was called Smith and Sons Stationery of Staines, or whatever, was important and that if they took the name away, they would lose customers. I told them that their customers wouldn't care what the name of the business was if the products were the right price and arrived on time, but they just couldn't see it.

It was such a missed opportunity. This was just before the internet took off and if we had had an online presence with a business which had a turnover of hundreds of millions of pounds, it would have been worth a fortune. We did manage to set up a founding members scheme, which offered a watered-down version of the idea, but it only attracted about 17 members and so it was eventually shut down.

Reluctantly, I decided that I was wasting my time banging my head against a brick wall. So I started an online office-supplies company myself.

Office supplies

I set up the business with two brothers, one of whom I had met at a cocktail party held by my brother Peter. I found a website developer in America, Tom Lahey, to build a website for us that could handle 40,000 products, but which could also load the pages fast enough to enable customers to navigate them quickly. This was back in the days of dial-up internet connections, so the website needed to be fast enough for people to use. I felt that a customer needed to be able to navigate from the front page to the product they wanted to buy in no more than three clicks.

We didn't want to ask friends and family for money to invest in the business until we were absolutely sure that we could create a website that would work, so the three of us each put in £50,000 to get the website built. When it was clear that it really would work, we raised £750,000 from friends and family and in 1999 we launched the business, calling it Euroffice.

It initially went well, and it was not long before we got a promise of £3m in venture capital from Barclays Private Equity on the condition that we found a lead investor with another £2m investment elsewhere. But before we managed to find the £2m the internet bubble burst and Barclays Private Equity withdrew their offer. Suddenly, we were running out of money fast.

Building a technology business is very capital intensive. The monthly 'burn', the amount you lose every month, is often in the tens of thousands of pounds. We were burning around £50,000 per month and the three of us weren't taking any salaries. Eventually we got to the point where we realised that we were insolvent and would have to close the business down. The brothers were pretty freaked out about being insolvent as it is technically illegal. However, if you have run your own business, you know as well as I do that sometimes you just have to do what needs to be done and get on with it. You can't always be whiter than white and occasionally you have to push the boundaries, sometimes even cross the line.

I pleaded with my business partners not to shut it down for a few more days, saying whether we went bust today or on Wednesday made little difference, while I tried to see if there was a solution. This went on for a few weeks. We just kept kicking the can down the road a few days at a time. I just knew instinctively that I could solve the problem but hadn't quite figured out how.

Eventually I had no choice but to go ask, or rather beg, my dad to help us out. He told me point blank that he wouldn't help any more. So my dad and I drove together from his house in Belgravia to our office by Putney Bridge. During that 30-minute trip he berated me on business and why he didn't want to support me anymore. I was OK with that. We arrived at our office and my dad went into a meeting room with the brothers to give them the bad news. I didn't think there was any point in me hearing it all again. Fifteen minutes later they came out and the brothers were beaming and hugging my dad. For some unknown reason, my dad had decided to step in and effectively save Euroffice.

He gave us a loan to tide us over for a few months, which turned out to be all I needed to find a long-term solution. I totally understand and appreciate the importance of him being able to do this. I'm very aware that not everyone can simply ask their dad for a loan to keep their business afloat and that, as a result, many businesses go under – often for the sake of just a few thousand pounds. If my dad hadn't helped us out, then the business would have been dealt a severe blow and that could have spelt the end of my entrepreneurial internet ambitions. Possibly the brothers might not be where they are today.

During the extra time my dad's investment had afforded us, I came up with the idea of doing invoice discounting, a process whereby we could sell our unpaid invoices on to a finance company, who would give us a percentage (often around 85%) of the amount that we were owed immediately, rather than having to wait weeks or months for the payments to come in. That gave us enough cash-flow liquidity to continue running the business and some months later we managed to secure a £1m investment from an Italian venture-capital investor called NetPartners, who also provided us with a £1m loan later on.

Euroffice began to build up sales but one big drawback of being one of the first internet-based businesses was that we had to spend a lot of time educating customers, because they simply weren't used to buying things this way. The search engine Google barely existed and there was no such thing as online marketing. So we decided to tackle the problem head on by building a field-sales operation consisting of a team of people who would go out visiting businesses and collecting their business cards or compliment slips. We sent all these business cards and email addresses to a chap called Tomas in Ethiopia, who in turn entered them into a database we could use for email marketing at scale. We would then email these potential customers with special offers to get them to try out our internet office-supplies business.

This worked well, but we still needed to get customers comfortable with the idea of actually ordering products on their computer. So our field-sales teams started going into businesses in person and offering to open up an account for them and help them place their first order. In those days, online credit-card payments were not common and if someone ordered office products online, they would expect to receive an invoice shortly afterwards and pay by cheque 30 days later. But this exposed the business to the potential problem of unpaid bills and bad debt. To solve this, I figured out a way to verify a customer's account within two hours of them placing an order to make sure that it was a legitimate business before we released their order for delivery the following day.

The way it worked was that a customer would place an order on the website. When asked if they wanted to pay by card or on account, 99% of businesses chose on account. So we asked them to open an account with us and give us their relevant details. We then said thank you for the order, it will be with you tomorrow and the invoice will be in the post with 30-days credit. As long as a customer placed the order before 5pm, we were able to deliver the goods the following day, a service all of the office-supplies wholesalers offered at the time.

When a new customer opened an account and placed their first order, we asked them to do so before 3pm to ensure guaranteed next-day delivery. In the two hours we had between 3pm and the delivery cut-off from the wholesalers at 5pm, we went to work on credit accessing the new customer's business.

We had a very good accountancy partner called CBS in St Albans and they were experts in credit scoring companies. Credit scoring is a system that assigns a credit score to a company based on their accounts and payments history. Based on all this information, a credit score was arrived at. If the score was 384 and above, that would translate into bad debt of around 1% for Euroffice, which we could live with. The real beauty of the system was that it was done completely behind the scenes and was mostly fully automated. The customer placed an order on account with 30-days credit, as was customary in the industry back then, and the goods were delivered the next day with free-of-charge delivery. Behind the scenes, we put the order aside until we had determined whether the credit risk was acceptable. If it was, we released the order in our system and it went to our wholesaler for drop shipment direct to the customer.

Sometimes you can't change customer behaviour overnight and if you fight it, you'll likely go out of business. Today, 20 years later, everybody pays by credit card online and the issue we were facing has disappeared.

LIFE LESSON

Always do whatever it takes to stay alive so you can fight another day.

Euroffice continued to grow, but sadly I soon realised that it wasn't going to be the kind of business that would ever be worth a huge amount of money. I just couldn't see how the three of us were going to get rich from the part of the company that wasn't owned by the Venture Capital Fund. So I reduced my involvement in the business by going part-time and started looking around for something else to do.

I left Euroffice completely in 2005 and the company was bought by a private-equity firm called Balderton Capital in late 2010. Our early friends and family investors doubled their money and the few investors that helped us out along with my dad quadrupled their investment. I sold all my shares and cashed in over £1m.

Chapter 4
The Birth Of XLN

ONE DAY I was having an account review meeting with CBS, the company that did the credit checking for Euroffice, and I got talking to the owner, Simon Paul. He was also chairman and a very large shareholder of Electricity Direct, the biggest independent electricity company at the time.

Simon mentioned, in passing, that he wanted to start a field-sales operation for ED and after he had elaborated on his plans, I told him that based on what he had told me, he was going to be spending £375 per new customer. He asked me how the hell I knew that, because it had taken KPMG three months to work that out. When I explained that field sales was exactly what I had been doing for the past 12 years, he asked me to build a field-sales operation for him. I agreed, on the condition that he gave me £60,000 to set it up and £50,000 a month for a minimum of six months to pay for salespeople and office overheads, and of course my fee.

All Simon wanted was to see a customer's existing electricity bill, so that he could then offer them a cheaper deal if they switched to his business instead. So I created a non-profit organisation called the Small Business Cost Advisory Service.

The Small Business Cost Advisory Service (SBCAS)

Once I had built the field-sales operation, my team would go round to businesses in the capacity of an 'independent non-profit cost advisory service' and ask them to show us their various utility bills in exchange for us giving them some impartial advice on how they could save money. Somewhat an analogue version of today's price-comparison websites.

I would get all these various utility bills ranging from council tax, business rates, office supplies, BT telephone bills, gas and electricity bills and other sundry invoices. The only bills I was really interested in were their electricity bill which I would fax daily to Simon's sales organisation. They, in turn, would contact the customer, produce a competitive electricity quote and send a salesman out to close the deal. The rest of the bills I threw in the bin. But then it dawned on me that for every electricity bill I got, I was getting four BT phone bills. I decided that there had to be some way of saving customers money on their phone bills as well as their electricity bills – especially since they all seemed to hate BT.

I thought that if Simon can make a business out of selling cheaper electricity to these people, and we were getting four times the number of phone bills as we were electricity bills, then why couldn't we supply them with cheaper phone calls?

Like an inventor staring at the same puzzle for months, finally the penny dropped and an idea that would change everything crystallized. And that is how the idea for XLN was born. It was born out of constantly moving, opening doors, getting involved, being ambitious and taking chances. You don't make your millions standing still. You have to get out there. The more situations you put yourself in, the higher the chances of the magic happening. The higher the chances of finding yourself in a situation that changes everything. There are business opportunities to be found in all areas of life, you just have to keep your eyes open in order to spot them. This was my lightbulb moment.

LIFE LESSON

The more you get to know your business, the easier it is to spot opportunities to make money. Sometimes ideas seem to come out of nowhere, but that's not true, they come from hard work, detailed observation, perseverance and being in the right place at the right time.

Chapter 5
Growing XLN

HAVING REALISED THAT there might be a gap in the market for a business which provided small companies with cheaper phone lines and calls, I decided that this was a business that I really wanted to start. I committed to investing £250,000 to get it off the ground.

What's in a name?

I find naming a new company quite a fun process. Likewise, coming up with a logo or corporate identity. Yes, I know it's kind of childish but nevertheless I find it fun. It is the birth of a company and this is the very first manifestation of what it will be. I do think you want the name and logo, if you want a logo, to properly reflect and project what you stand for and what the business is about. Sometimes that is not possible, and sometimes you need the name to help in aspects of the company's operations. Clearly, that is not the fashion nowadays, as most companies seem to favour some funky and entirely arbitrary name.

The great thing about having a business name made up of three letters is that you can use it in all sorts of ways – I knew from day one that XLN would have to grow by way of a field-sales force, so I needed a name that sounded good when I was recruiting salespeople.

Field sales is pretty much 50% recruitment, so I decided to choose a company name that I could describe as 'The XYZ Opportunity'. Also, remember, I had previously been involved with a company called XPD, which I liked the simplicity of, so that was my starting point. So, I started with an X and wanted three letters. I started playing with various permutations of X-- Telecom and after only a couple of hours I had settled on XLN Telecom. Obviously telecoms had to feature in the name, because it never occurred to me that we might do other products one day. It made sense at the time, but in hindsight I should probably have left that out. Today, we just call the company XLN.

Many people have asked me where the name came from, what it means and so forth. It isn't a shortened form of excellent and it doesn't mean XL Nellemann (Tom Oliver came up with that very silly one). It honestly doesn't mean anything. I just thought it would sound great as 'The XLN Opportunity' because that was how I was going to pitch it to potential commission-only salespeople. Simple as that.

Curiously, a number of years ago one of my very best field-sales managers, Steven Pun, came into my office beaming and exclaimed that he now knew why I had called the company XLN. I asked, mildly surprised, why that was? He said that he'd been rummaging around in one of the storage rooms in our office building and had found the original number plate for my first Ferrari, which I had bought some seven years before I started XLN. I had never noticed it before because I had put a personalised number plate on the car as soon as I had acquired it. But the original number plate read C699 XLN. Serendipity I suppose, but it did make me wonder. Maybe things are just meant to be. Still spooky though.

I planned to establish the new telecom business on my own. However, when we started Euroffice, the two brothers and I had agreed that we were in business together as equal partners for all our ventures – no matter what the opportunity might be. I didn't want to turn my back on the agreement, so although I funded this new venture myself (with my dad's financial help) and was the only one working full-time on it, they both had a 25% share of the business and so did my dad. Four equal partners.

Once I realised that my idea could potentially work, the first step was to work out how to actually become a telecoms business and supply phonelines to customers. It was around 2002; at this point, BT pretty much had a monopoly over the sector and were suppling all the landlines in the country. People were talking about deregulation in principle, but it hadn't actually kicked in yet. So I needed to work out how I could get cheaper landline prices from BT.

At the time, BT offered a product which provided cheaper prices for big businesses that had lots of different branches. If, for example, you were Marks & Spencer, who had 4,000 shops across the country and spent over £1m annually on phone bills, you could buy phone calls at much lower rates than if you were just a small business with one or two phone lines. In those days, a small business would pay 2.95 pence for a local call, whereas if you were a business spending £1m a year, you would pay 1.37 pence per minute.

That was a big difference in price. So I got in touch with BT and asked them if it mattered whether I actually owned the 4,000 shops that I would be paying the phone bills for. And after a while, they came back to me and said no, they didn't think so. I realised that as long as I committed to spending over £1m a year with BT, I could get these really low rates and sell them onto my customers and make some money out of it. If they were currently paying 2.95 pence per minute, then I could sell my calls to them at 2 pence, for example, and still make a 30% margin. My plan was starting to come together.

Partnership: The arrival of OneBill

Then another one of those unexpected and transformational moments happened. Before I had a chance to get a deal with BT set up, a man called Mike Thornley contacted me. He told me that he had started a telecoms business in Worthing called OneBill Telecom, which supplied businesses with phonelines and calls, and that he already had around 4,000 customers. I told him that I was starting a similar business providing phonelines and calls myself, and that I would be building it using field sales. I explained that it was going to be really big.

At some point, Mike told me that getting 10,000 customers would be pretty much the limit of what I could achieve, and that it would be impossible to grow beyond 20,000 customers. Certainly, no-one had ever achieved anything bigger than that.

Mike is a great businessman and we got on really well. Eventually, we agreed that we would form a partnership. I would secure the sales under my brand XLN and with my tariffs, and then I would pass the customers over to him to do all the paperwork, billing and customer service, and arrange for BT to switch each customer's phoneline over to us. I felt that in the early stages of starting the business, particularly one as complicated as this, I wanted to focus on the things that really moved the needle, which in this case was sales, so it made perfect sense to outsource the other bits.

I agreed with Mike upfront that the customers would ultimately be mine – we wouldn't own them together – but that we would split the margin we made on each deal. I also made it clear that his company was effectively providing a service for my company, and that at some point I would leave him and do it all on my own. I strongly believe in being completely upfront and transparent with business partners. For a partnership to be truly successful, you must work hard to find a win-win solution that works equally well for both parties.

Mike liked the idea of a partnership. He wanted more sales and could see that this was an opportunity to get them, and as he was already doing customer service and billing and all of these things, he would be able to make extra money from essentially the same system.

So we agreed to work together, with no money changing hands, and it worked very well. By this time, the WLR (wholesale line rental) market had been developed. Consequently, every time we got a new customer, we would send a card with some information on it to BT and they would switch that connection from their system onto ours. Instead of BT billing the customer, they would bill us and we would in turn bill our new business customer.

The only problem was that BT obviously didn't want to do this; they were only doing it because they were being required to by law. They constantly tried to put every obstacle possible in our way; they would delay making the switch, or they would suddenly update their systems overnight without telling anyone so that our system wouldn't then work. BT, it seemed, would do whatever they could to frustrate, delay, annoy and hinder us. Even when we complained to the telecoms regulator, Ofcom, nothing would change. In those days, Ofcom had very little power to force BT to comply. In fact, we used to joke that it was called BT Ofcom because it so often sided with BT. It was an ongoing battle that never seemed to get any easier.

We started the business in Vauxhall, in the same office block as Euroffice was based, but I soon moved it into the first floor of a dilapidated building where we created the classic start-up vibe with exposed brickwork and makeshift furniture. That wasn't just for show though. In the beginning, I had no idea how well the business would do, so I was determined not to waste money unnecessarily. I would hustle and haggle to save a pound here and a pound there and would aim to negotiate a 20–30% discount on everything I bought. I even hung the low voltage lighting in the ceiling myself. Probably a good thing I never became an electrician.

As the chart below shows, this frugal approach soon paid off. The business grew and grew until eventually we ended up taking over the entire building as well as half of another building. It was a huge rabbit warren of offices on all different floors and levels.

Fiscal year-end figures 2003-2009

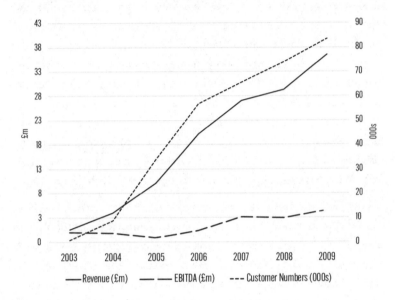

—— Revenue (£m)   — — EBITDA (£m)   - - - Customer Numbers (000s)

LIFE LESSON

Growing a business is complex and a lot of hard work. Great work habits are everything. Diligence, relationship management, enthusiasm, positivity, and a brain that never stops thinking, 'how can we do this better?' is essential.

Chapter 6
How To Get Rich Quick... Again

IN THIS FIRST stage of operations, we were simply offering cheaper landlines and phone calls, but that was more than enough to drive our growth. To create a successful business, you only need to have an initial idea and a concept. You can trial it on a small scale and then, if it works, you can scale it up – by adding more salespeople, for example. The secret is to get the initial execution of the idea and the metrics right, because if it will work with one salesperson, it will likely work with 200 of them.

As a commodity business, we knew we had to be the cheapest provider in the market, otherwise we might as well pack up and go home. People might have hated BT, but that alone wasn't going to be enough to persuade them to switch. We knew we had to win them on price and then keep them with quality service.

LIFE LESSON

Get the business model right while you are small and have both feet on the ground. Then scale the hell out of it. That's the quickest way to reach your goals.

A different approach

From the start, I decided to pay our salespeople in a different way than the rest of the industry. At that time, most salespeople were paid something called a 'residual' every time they made a sale, which was a little commission on what the customer had signed up to spend on a monthly basis. If a customer spent £50 a month, for example, then the salesperson might get £5 a month for every month that the customer stayed with the business.

In my mind, there were two problems with this arrangement. The first was that customers were spending an average of £40 a month with XLN, rather than £500, which meant that if we were paying £5 of that to the salesperson as a residual, it would take someone who was working solely on commission a very long time to sign up enough customers to provide them with an income they could live off.

The second problem was that once our best sales managers had built up a big sum of residuals that paid out every month, there was little incentive for them to keep on working really hard to sign up new customers. They could get to a point where they would be getting an income of £5,000 or £6,000 a month from residuals and then decide that they didn't really need to go to work. Eventually they would have to get more customers to replace customers who left, but there could potentially be quite a long time in the middle when they could coast and when all the good work habits they had learned would fade away.

I just couldn't see how I was going to be able to grow a big sales force in this way, with half my salespeople unable to earn a living wage and the other half earning so much that they didn't need to work. It didn't quite tally with the sales system I had learnt in America and subsequently perfected over ten years in the UK.

So I began to pay our salespeople an upfront fee for every customer they signed up instead. Rather than giving them £5 a month forever, I would give them a one-off fee of £60. Our salespeople liked it because they got more money in the short term, and I liked it because the minute they stopped selling, they would stop earning, which kept them working and producing and maintaining good work habits. It was an arrangement that benefited both parties. Very quickly, the whole industry changed to paying their salespeople in this way, because it was so much simpler.

Another thing I was looking into was how to create some innovative tariffs with price points that might attract customers' interest. One day, the idea came to me that we could offer a tariff that included line rental and 300 inclusive local and national minutes for £12.99 a month, when BT was charging £13.72 just for the line rental. We called the tariff Light Plus. I knew that we wouldn't make much money out of it, but I realised that it would be a great way of getting customers to sign up. We could then make money on the calls customers made to mobiles, which weren't included in the deal and which in those days cost about 25p a minute.

The economics and my thinking at the time went something like this: the line rental from BT Wholesale cost us £9.99 per month and the minutes cost 1.37 pence per minute. Alas, if the customer ended up using more than 219 minutes of the 300 free inclusive minutes, we would lose money on a monthly basis. However, we had gathered enough data and experience to know that the average number of minutes used across all our customers on a monthly basis was only 203 minutes. It was going to be a close-run thing, but I was confident we would break even and then we could make money on the mobile calls. But the most important reason behind it was that I was hoping the tariff would be a hit and gain us lots of new customers. Increasing the customer base was critical to averaging out the fixed overheads of the business.

Our salespeople loved the tariff because it was such a simple pitch – customers would pay a slightly lower price than BT charged, but with us they would get 300 minutes for free, an additional saving of up to £10 per month. It was the first all-inclusive tariff in the UK; it felt new and fresh.

Fortunately, it turned out that customers loved the Light Plus tariff too. Our sales almost doubled overnight, rising from 375 to 700 in a week. It was the first time I had ever had a proper home run on a product launch, and it felt fantastic.

But because we paid our salespeople on commission only and were paying them upfront rather than each month, our sales costs also doubled overnight. Suddenly, I needed to find an extra £80,000 a month to pay the additional sales commissions. It was a complete shock. When I was at university, I had been taught that a business could be so successful that it would fail because it didn't have enough cash flow, but it never really made much sense to me. Now I understood what that meant.

I asked one of the brothers to calculate how much money we would need to cover the gap before all the new customers started generating enough profits and we would be back to positive cash flows. He said we needed £150,000. So I crawled on my knees to my dad and asked him if he could lend us the money. Thankfully, he was really helpful and said, "yes, absolutely no problem".

The problem was that the brother had miscalculated, so I had to go back every month for six months to ask my dad to lend us more money to tide us over. When we finally broke even again, we had borrowed the enormous sum of £850,000 from him. Fortunately, my dad was pretty cool about it. We would probably have gone out of business otherwise.

I know what you are thinking – I had promised myself that I wasn't going to ask my dad for money anymore, yet there I was asking for nearly £1m to get me out of trouble. But I figured that if my business was a success then this £1m would help create many more millions of pounds, so I decided that it was worth breaking my pledge, just this once. We paid my dad a commercial interest rate and were able to pay him back in full including interest within a year. I will forever be grateful to him for having supported me in so many different ways throughout my career.

LIFE LESSON

No matter how promising your business becomes, cash flow is king and if you get it wrong it can kill your company. Make cash-flow management a priority. And remember to choose your parents carefully!

Chapter 7
The Birth Of Brilliant Customer Service

M EANWHILE, WE WERE continuing to sign up new customers. In the first year of being in business we got 800 customers and in year two we got about 8,000 new customers. I kept telling Mike Thornley that he needed to hire more customer-service people to handle the calls, because we were going to get another 20,000 customers in year three. But I don't think he believed me, because I was basically saying that we were going to do twice the number of sales in a year that he had done in three years. So he wasn't particularly willing or keen to invest a lot of money in more people and systems. In the end, we grew by 25,000 customers that year.

I totally understand why, but the consequence was that the service levels we offered to our customers deteriorated. We simply didn't have enough people to serve the growing number of customers we were signing up. The service levels weren't brilliant in the first place and when the wheels started falling off, we quickly had to decide what to do.

The solution was to start taking on some of the customer-facing functions ourselves, such as credit control and provisioning. I would have loved to have left the operations with Mike for a while longer, but it just wasn't possible. Mike was running a great business, but we were just growing too fast for him. Inevitably, the day had come when I had to tell Mike that we could pretty much survive on our own now, and that it was time for us to part ways.

We added up the accounts, paid him what he was owed, and shook hands as friends. It was a good partnership that served us both well for a few very crucial years but it was time to go it alone.

India calling

Now that we were handling all the customer-facing functions ourselves, XLN started growing even faster. We got to the point where we simply couldn't hire people quick enough to be able to grow our customer-service teams as fast as we needed to, so I decided to outsource our customer service to a call centre in Kolkata, India.

However, over the next few years I began to realise that the culture, mentality and daily reality of life in India was so hugely different to that in the UK that having our customer-service operations in Kolkata simply didn't work.

For a start, the big difference in the value of money was a problem. If a customer rang me to complain about a phone call on their bill for £4.60 that they supposedly never made, for example, then instead of wasting a lot of time trying to get to the bottom of it, I would just credit the amount back to their account and explain that in the future we couldn't keep doing this. But in India, £5 represents roughly a day's salary. It's a lot of money there and so understandably they didn't feel comfortable crediting that amount of money to a customer. Hence, they would hesitate and eventually get a manager involved which would take a lot of time and provide a poor customer experience. It would actually end up costing more in admin time than the credit was worth.

The other problem was that because India is so populous, jobs in call centres are in great demand. The owners and managers, therefore, hold quite a lot of sway over the workers and fire them at will if they don't do well. As a result, the people answering the phones follow the operational manual to the letter because they can't afford to lose their jobs.

This rigid adherence to the script and fear-based management style caused quite a lot of problems. I once listened to a call from one of our customers who rang to say that she needed to terminate her husband's office line because he had recently passed away. The issue should have been dealt with quickly and sensitively but instead the call-centre worker asked the customer if she could send a letter confirming that her husband had died.

Not surprisingly, the customer was really upset. The problem was that the operational manual said that, if an agent wasn't actually speaking to the account holder then they needed to get the request in writing. No call-centre worker would dare to deviate from that rule because he or she might have lost their job.

There were many examples of this kind of thing happening and I realised that this approach was common practice everywhere. I kept hearing these kind of horror stories from other businesses too. That type of fear-based management just doesn't lend itself to all the grey areas of empowering employees to give great customer service. I loved the people and the team we had developed in India but from a business point of view it just wasn't working. I knew that I needed to rip up the manual. I wanted to do it differently and I wanted to change the industry because, more than anything else, I wanted my customers to have a great experience.

There was one other important motivation too. I had decided that we needed to sell more products than just phone calls and broadband in the future, and that we could become the first business to provide a range of utilities to small businesses. However, in order for us to have legitimacy in trying to sell our customers another product, our service would have to be first class right from the very first moment a prospective customer heard about XLN. If we weren't brilliant with our core product, it would be impossible for us to ask our customers to buy another service from us. We needed to be able to say, look, we are the best at this by a country mile, we are still the cheapest and now we can offer you other products that can save you time, money, hassle and aggravation.

So we shut down our operation in India and outsourced part of our customer-service operation to a very reputable company in Selkirk, Scotland. It was really expensive and, in the end, didn't work out for similar quality reasons. Then we tried, once more, to build a bigger customer-service team in London, but that didn't work because the turnover rate of the people we employed was too high. We simply couldn't get our people's skillset to the level that we needed it to be.

It takes around six months for an agent to learn our products and systems and, within a year, most agents in London wanted to move on to bigger and better things. Even if we paid top salaries to our experienced agents, it really wasn't enough for a decent existence in London and therefore all the great agents would leave for another career. Customer-service jobs, however well paid, seemed to be an entry-level job for many people and we really needed them to stay for years to be able to offer world-class customer service.

Eventually, I decided that the only way to get this right was to get as hands-on with customer service as I am with sales and bring it all in-house. So we conducted a study of 20 cities based on lots of different factors, such as the size of the population, the availability of transport links, how many other call centres were located there, whether there was a university there and so on. Based on the study's findings, I decided to build a state-of-the-art workplace for 200 people in Sheffield, where people would actually view customer service as a proper career.

The call centre we built there works brilliantly. It took us a long time to get it right and it certainly wasn't for lack of trying. It doesn't matter if you don't get something right the first time. There is no shame in trying something out that doesn't work. What does matter is sticking with something when it is clear that it doesn't work but you know you can make a success of it. Make your mistakes, learn from them, and then move on quickly.

LIFE LESSON

Keep going until you find the solution that's right for your business. Don't give up - even if it's proving much harder than you initially thought. You win by taking the harder path and continuously improving what you're doing. Dream big and set your targets higher than you think possible, then commit completely to its eventual attainment. It's always better to shoot for the stars - if you miss, you might just hit the moon.

Chapter 8
Selling The Business

B Y 2007, THE world economy was booming. XLN was on track for making profits of about £3m that year, which meant that the business was worth about £25m. That was a lot of money tied up in one place. I suggested that we should take some chips off the table, because if the market crashed it could be another five years before we got an opportunity to get any money out. And to be honest, I wasn't at all sure that the business would be around five years later, let alone survive a crash.

The brothers agreed to sell the business, so we hired an advisor from KPMG, Neil Conaghan, to conduct the sales process for us. He turned out to be a really great corporate finance guy, which was a huge relief, because selling a business to private equity is one of the more stressful things you can do in your life.

It's full on, 18 hours a day for a six-month period and some of it under a lot of stress and pressure. There are people crawling all over you doing technical due diligence, legal due diligence, financial due diligence, commercial due diligence and so on, and you still have to make sure the business is performing. Your management team can easily get distracted from the day-to-day running of the business and that can mean that your 'current trading' starts falling off, which often means that the buyer starts chipping away at the price or indeed walks away.

It is really hard-core and very intense.

We saw a number of potential buyers, mainly private-equity firms, and ended up doing a management-buyout deal in January 2008 with a newly-formed private-equity firm called Zeus, now called Palatine. They took a majority stake in the business in return for an investment of around £10m.

Private Equity

The way private equity (PE) works is that if you are running the business, you take half your money out and leave the other half in. From time to time, private equity gets bad publicity because of the odd bad apple in the barrel. My experience with PE has been very positive from an operational point of view. The change that they instigated and the improvements a business typically achieves are impressive. In terms of governance, process improvements and management structure, the changes were huge and transformational for us. There is no way that XLN would be the amazing company it is today without the expert input from three fantastic private-equity houses.

The valuation we agreed for the business was £28m, which meant that my stake was worth £7m – a huge amount of money to me. I managed to hold on to roughly the same stake in the business because I got some additional equity, known as sweet equity or sweat equity, for staying on as CEO. Frankly, I never thought I would see any more money from the business, I was just happy with what I got out. As part of the deal, one of the brothers sold his equity stake and left the business but the other brother joined the business full-time. My dad kept his stake in the business.

Of course, nothing is ever without a bit of a drama, and this was no exception. The original exit plan was that brother number one and I were going to run the business. As part of that agreement, he insisted that he wanted to be CEO and, since I've never been too hung up on titles, I agreed. Then one day, as we were preparing for management presentations with the team at KPMG, one of the partners made this fatal statement to the brother: "It's fine that you become CEO, but Christian will always be XLN." The following day, the brother announced that he didn't want to be part of the management buy-out.

Holy mackerel, what a curveball that was – and literally days before we were due to present a united front to potential buyers. I really didn't see that coming. But these things happen; that's just life and business. So, on to plan B, which of course we didn't have. I immediately arranged a meeting with brother number two, who was supposed to have left the business as part of the sale process, with the clear objective of talking him into staying and running the business with me. Again, titles were the main subject of discussion and as part of the compromise we arrived at, he became co-CEO of the business.

Zeus turned out to be the ideal investor for the business. They were a PE firm that got behind and understood founders and entrepreneurs – which was important to me – and I had a brilliant relationship with them. Their approach was to continue running the business in the way it had been run but to put some structure around it. So it was a step up but it wasn't a complete change of style. I spoke to one of the partners, Tony Dickin, at least every other day and always sought his advice. I never took it for granted that I couldn't be replaced as CEO of the business, but they were really pleased with the progress that XLN was making.

One of the great things we did with Zeus on board was to buy OneBill, the business that I had partnered with when we first started out. It was a close-run thing, however. By the time I found out that it was for sale, Mike, who still owned it, was all lined up to sell the business to his management team. He had practically agreed a deal and was also about to go on holiday.

I knew that buying OneBill would be a great opportunity for our business and one that I couldn't afford to miss out on. But I had no time to waste. I couldn't afford to wait two weeks until Mike got back from holiday because the deal might have been done by then, and I knew that I had to speak to him face to face to try to convince him to sell to me. I had to act now, and I had to act fast. This could be a real game changer.

So I quickly got in the car and drove down to meet him. I asked him how much he wanted for the business and after some discussion we agreed a price and shook hands on it. The deal was done, and it was a win-win for both of us.

I left that meeting knowing that I had a monumental task in front of me, in the form of integrating the businesses and moving all the customers, about 20,000, onto our CRM (customer record management) and billing systems. I also knew it could be a transformational deal financially, and one that Palatine would be happy with; meanwhile, Mike had walked away a multimillionaire. Not a bad start to his holiday and a great full-circle event of how we started our relationship some six years earlier.

LIFE LESSON

Sometimes you just have to go for it. You have to trust your instincts, and just make the bloody decision. Seize opportunities when they present themselves because they may not come again and then figure out how to make it work.

Because Mike and I had worked well together, and critically we had ended our working relationship on a good, clean and fair note, I had the opportunity to buy his business. If that hadn't been the case, I'm convinced Mike would never have sold his company to me, at any price. We're still good friends to this day and remain in contact.

The stress mounts

In December 2008, I bought a house on an acre plot of land in Sunningdale. The idea was to tear the house down and build my own home for my young family, something that had always been a dream of mine. But in January 2009, the financial system was starting to fall apart completely – the great financial crisis was beginning to gather pace. It was to become an extremely stressful time.

I had, as you always tend to do with houses, overextended myself a bit. I was also in the middle of trying to close on the £11m acquisition of OneBill. For the first time in my life, I had a week of absolute insomnia. It felt as though I was going mad. I tried progressively more radical things to try and fall asleep, and I finally succeeded on the Friday.

Becoming successful may look fabulously exciting from the outside, but on the inside, it can feel immensely stressful and occasionally overwhelming. You are not only making decisions involving enormous sums of money, but you are also continually trying to hit targets, deliver on promises and achieve everything that is expected of you. On top of that, you have a responsibility to hundreds of staff on your shoulders as well as your own family's future. That week, I felt the full force of it all and almost fell apart.

Bringing OneBill into XLN enabled us to benefit from many synergies and we were able to take a lot of costs out of the acquired business. As a result, we more than tripled our annual profits from £3m to £11m in less than three years. It felt like an extraordinary achievement. Just a few years earlier, I had been borrowing money to keep the business afloat and now we were preparing to sell the company again.

But it hadn't been entirely without drama and at times Zeus had shown its ruthless side. One of the consequences of promising brother number two the position of co-CEO was that he took it to mean that he didn't have to pay any notice to what I had to say. We were, of course, equal partners and thus at the same level, but that shouldn't put an end to collaboration. He wanted to be the boss, or at least his own boss, so he started to build little fiefdoms with the teams he managed. It was becoming increasingly disruptive.

Zeus made the decision that they wanted him out, which caused me concern and presented a big dilemma for me. As I mentioned earlier, we had in the early days of Euroffice agreed to be equal partners for the long run. Hence, I couldn't support him being booted out of the company. We eventually settled on a compromise whereby he saved face and his title and became CEO of OneBill, and I became Group CEO with full responsibility over the entire group of companies.

Zeus (or Palatine, as they are now known) sold their stake in our business in October 2010 to another private-equity firm, ECI Partners, making 4.5 times their initial investment. It is still the most successful investment they have made to date. I should mention that XLN was their second ever investment and that they are now raising funds for their fourth PE fund. Tony Dickin, Gary Tipper and Ed Fazakerley have been phenomenally successful because they have stuck to their guns and backed only successful entrepreneurs to help them scale and improve their companies. I'm still in touch with Tony and Gary on a regular basis, and often help with due diligence on potential new telecom acquisitions. I have invested in their three funds and am considering, as I write, investing in the fourth.

Private equity is not for everyone. If an entrepreneur has treated their business like their own personal fiefdom, only turning up when it suited them, then they are going to get a shock. Private-equity investors don't want to run businesses and they certainly don't want to change a founding CEO, but if that is the only option, they won't hesitate. The way you survive private equity is by delivering; if you don't deliver, you will be in trouble.

Fortunately, I have always worked all the hours in a day, so getting involved with private equity made absolutely no difference to me. They would say, let's do a 100-day plan and I would say yes fine, we do that anyway – and we don't just do the first 100 days of an investment period, we do it all the time.

For XLN and myself, getting private equity on board was a good idea for many reasons. To start with, it is always helpful to work with and be surrounded by smart people who potentially have a different viewpoint or approach, and private equity is, by and large, run by really smart people. They bring a lot of practical experience, are very well connected, and can suggest a lot of options. Private-equity investors are particularly good with banks and financing, because they know who to speak to, and they are very good if you want to do an acquisition, because they have already done a lot of them and know what to look for. I learnt a lot of things from them.

And there has been another unexpected benefit. When Palatine sold the business to ECI Partners, I hired the same corporate finance guy, Neil Conaghan from KPMG, to advise me personally. When the deal was completed, I managed to persuade Neil to come on board and help me grow XLN as our group chief financial officer. He has been here almost nine years now and is my right-hand man.

In business, you need to surround yourself with smart people who can provide a different point of view and, importantly, can support you in areas where you might not be so strong. I brought in some extremely talented people over the next few years, starting with Neil. We also bought out brother number two at more than twice the value of the first deal.

——— LIFE LESSON ———

Don't be afraid of working with smart people who challenge you daily and whose abilities complement your own. The worst thing you can do is surround yourself with 'yes men' that have similar skills and personalities to you.

Chapter 9
Growing Pains

OUR NEW PRIVATE-EQUITY investors, ECI Partners, invested on a valuation of £77m. When they came on board, we knew that the business had to 'grow up' – we needed to build a proper management structure so that XLN could one day run without me. At the time, I pretty much directed everything, and it was clear that if I wasn't there, the business would have collapsed. So, we started putting more structure into the business, adding senior management, middle management, more robust systems, processes, governance and so on.

But by then, it had become clear that we had a big problem with the way we were running the sales side of XLN. It was no longer working as it was supposed to and it wasn't fit for the future ambitions of the business.

Changing the structure

We had always hired salespeople on a commission-only basis, because that was the way that I had started out and frankly it was a system I was comfortable with from my perfume days. It was also a less risky way of scaling a large sales organisation, as the company wasn't on the hook for huge salary bills with little guarantee of individual sales performance.

As I mentioned earlier, our system worked like this. We would recruit people to join the organisation and they would spend an initial 90 days with us in a fast-track management programme. In the first 30 days, our recruits learn about the product, how to work the field correctly, great work habits and the culture of the business. After these 30 days of selling, we teach our recruits how to train and develop a few recently joined sales agents. Next, our salespeople are taught how to manage and motivate a team of their own. Usually, this phase takes between 30 and 60 days. Finally, we start teaching them how to run a sales operation independently. They would learn how to interview; how to recruit, hire and fire people; and how to run the administrative side of a sales office.

After about six months, during which time a salesperson would have earned a meagre wage only from the sales they had completed, XLN would give them a business of their own, investing in a new sales office for them somewhere in the country and kitting it out with furniture and training rooms. We would also provide them with everything they needed to operate a business, including all the materials and phone systems.

So, within six months of joining XLN, they would effectively be running their own business. And if they had learnt what we had taught them well, they would be able to start recruiting a team of their own and start earning a good income. It was the same way that I had set up the perfume business, and the objective was to open as many of these offices as we could. The 'owner' would then, in turn, manage between ten and 20 salespeople in their assigned area.

The problem was that some people would join XLN and go through the training process but not put enough effort in. So they wouldn't be successful and they would leave because they weren't making enough money. And then they would blame XLN and say it was all our fault. We were very open and transparent about the fact that it would be incredibly hard work, but that did not stop people complaining if they failed.

These complaints were initially manageable, because if people didn't like our system they would just go away and grumble to themselves, but when the internet and social media emerged, some of these people would go and write awful things on forums and blogs about how we were running a scam, and that we were taking advantage of poor deprived young people. Soon there were too many people bad-mouthing the company and it just became an untenable situation.

A long time ago in a sales office far far away

We had two other problems that were related to this. First, because we had a lot of offices – many of them far away – there were opportunities for the people running them to become somewhat untrustworthy. It was difficult to manage them from a distance, after all. Second, some of our managers wouldn't train the people they recruited well enough, so the quality of the training became inconsistent, or would sadly recruit people in an outright dishonest way.

When I was running the field-sales operation, I was always completely upfront about all aspects of the opportunity – the money was dire during training and many wouldn't make it to an office. However, most accepted that, rolled up their sleeves and became successful.

I realised that we couldn't solve the issue of quality inconsistency in hiring, training and HR matters as long as we let individuals recruit and train their own salespeople without supervision. The problem was that we couldn't supervise them because these offices were all over the country. But even if we were able to do that, the commission-only structure meant that in order to attract decent, high-quality people to the business and for them to be willing to put in the effort for four to six months, while earning very little money, there had to be a decent carrot at the end.

I had started out working on commission only. I worked hard and there was a pot of gold waiting for me at the end of the rainbow. The problem we had always faced was that if people didn't put the effort in, then the pot of gold wouldn't be there. And then they would blame us on social media, using the most disagreeable language, and I just knew that we could never overcome that. It was very disheartening because we were always clear about the opportunity we offered, and what it would take to be successful, but it is in some people's nature to blame everybody else but themselves.

The relentless unfounded criticism on social media was affecting our ability to recruit new salespeople and even employees for other departments. By the end of 2010, I'd had enough. I realised that our model didn't work anymore and that there was nothing I could do to stop people writing about us. I had a company and a reputation to protect, and our private-equity investors, ECI Partners, also had a gilt-edged reputation to look after.

So I shut down the entire field-sales operation pretty much overnight. We closed every single one of the 20 offices we had opened and got rid of all the people working in them, which amounted to over 100 salespeople. I was gutted.

Suddenly, we didn't have anyone selling our products and our business started to go backwards. We were losing 1,000 customers every month through natural churn and yet we had no way of replacing them because we didn't have any field salespeople signing new customers up. I was looking down the barrel of a gun.

Our only option was to try and create a new sales machine based entirely on salaries and a more normal compensation structure. We started recruiting new salespeople, but it took time to train them up. And because we were now paying them a salary, it took time to figure out how the new model worked.

If you have a commission-only model, you don't have to worry about productivity, because if your salespeople don't sell anything, you don't pay them. And we didn't have to worry about the costs per sale because there weren't really any fixed costs to speak of. We had some fixed overheads, but we didn't pay for sales that didn't happen. On the other hand, we had a lot of motivational issues, because if people didn't manage to sell anything on a particular day, then they would lose their confidence and attitude. So we were constantly trying to motivate our salespeople and talk them out of quitting their jobs.

Another issue with a commission-only model is the quality of the sales experience. When salespeople are desperate to earn money and/or are struggling to meet targets, there is a risk that they start embellishing the truth. In other words, they start lying to customers about the capabilities of the product or the pricing. They would offer discounts that weren't available and so the customers would, rightly, be upset when the invoice showed a different amount to what had been promised and agreed at the point of sale. That was another aspect that was incompatible with the kind of business I wanted to run.

When you move to a salary model, however, you are paying people whether or not they achieve any sales and so your customer-acquisition costs go through the roof. Now you don't have to motivate people to stay but you do have to motivate and manage their sales performance as well as the quality of the sales they are doing. So the whole structure is turned completely upside down. We had to figure out and re-engineer everything we did in order to manage these issues.

Consistency, consistency, consistency

The part that I was most unhappy with was the inconsistent quality of the people managers were hiring and the training that they were providing. You might have a great office with great salespeople who would do well and make money, but then you could also have a poor office with poor salespeople who wouldn't do well and wouldn't make money. I wanted consistency in training and recruitment, so when we closed down the entire sales channel we started recruiting and training people centrally. This way, we could control every part of the process ourselves. I would teach the trainers, and they would go on to instruct everyone else. I was invested in building the right culture from day one.

Now that we were employing people directly and without regional sales offices, we needed to find a way to control the salespeople who were scattered all over the country when we no longer had daily face-to-face contact with them.

This total transformation of the way we ran the field-sales organisation was the right thing to do, but the whole transition process took much longer than I thought it would. It was also a lot more complicated and painful than I had ever imagined.

When ECI Partners had invested in the business, I told them that making these changes was the right thing to do because it was the only way to succeed in the long term. But after four years, the business still wasn't quite where it needed to be and ECI Partners were coming towards the end of their investment horizon. I knew that the only way to really succeed was to start investing a significant amount of our own money into the business, and that you sometimes can't do that while being backed by private equity because they need the company's profits to keep going up, not down. Certainly, it didn't quite fit with their investment period.

When ECI invested back in October 2010, XLN was making EBITDA of around £11m; by the end of 2014, we had grown that to £17m. Neil and I discussed this at length and both agreed that the company needed a period of 3–4 years of heavy investment. We needed to sacrifice profits for a meaningful period of time in order to get every part of the company into world-class shape.

As a result, in November 2014, I bought back ECI's stake in the business myself at a company valuation of £133m with the help of GSO Capital Partners, the credit arm of Blackstone, who agreed to lend me £115m on the condition that I left all my money in the business. When they exited, the deal gave ECI a great return of three times their investment.

We then invested between £4m and £5m in the business every year for the next few years. Suddenly, this was a high-stakes game where initial leverage of 7.5 times had increased to almost ten times. I effectively gambled more than £17m of my own money on buying back the business. I could have lost every penny, but I was willing to take the risk because I wanted to see it through and I felt that I knew what needed to be done.

XLN's turnover stagnated and then declined for four years in a row; instead of making profits, we were piling up net losses. But finally, in 2017, the business broke even, and in 2018, it showed slight growth. By 2019, we were back on track, with good growth.

It took us a long time, but the company is now as big as it was when we embarked on our restructuring, and it is growing. We now have a team of people spread out across the country who each have their own territory to sell to, and the model is still similar in that, when they can demonstrate good work habits which translate into decent results, we allow them to start training and then managing other people.

But the difference now is that they are all employed directly by XLN on a salary, and they all report to us. We speak to them every morning and use technology to keep in touch and monitor their performance. We support all that activity with a range of teams that oversee verification, sales support, training and recruitment. I used to have five mid-level managers that reported to me, but now my leadership team is comprised of around 40 mid-level managers and seven senior-level managers.

It has been immensely hard work getting to this point, but it has been worth it. XLN now has a secure and solid sales, management and operational structure that will take the business anywhere it wants to go. The foundations are in place and they are unshakeable.

Our turnover is now £70m a year, we make EBITDA of £21m a year, and XLN is valued at around £250m. These figures are forecast to grow strongly over the next few years as the business settles into its new structure and shows what it is really capable of. We are also adding new product areas all the time – having started out simply offering cheap phonelines and calls, XLN now offer small businesses an entire range of utilities, including broadband, fibre, Wi-Fi, gas, electricity, and card payments. The sky really is the limit.

Meanwhile, somewhat to my surprise, I find that despite all the hard work and ridiculous hours, despite all the sacrifices, I have somehow also managed to create a wonderful life outside of the business. There is a huge price to pay for the kind of success I've had, and it can be easy to neglect the needs of family and friends – as the priorities of the business come first – or even to let life pass you by altogether. Fortunately, after years of working all the hours there are, I am now in a position where I can try to learn to enjoy both. Being able to leave the office early one day a week to collect my sons from school and spend time with them teaching them about the world before bedtime is one of the great new joys of my life.

LIFE LESSON

The greater the risk, the greater the reward. As the business grows, so do the risks, the stresses and the impact of your actions. You have to learn to trust your gut and dig in. If what you are doing is the right thing and you believe in it, the results will come.

Chapter 10
Giving Back

S O FAR IN this book I have only really focused on the machine; the sales structure and the model. But XLN is so much more than that. The brand is founded on one key principle – to be on the side of the embattled small-business owner where others simply aren't.

Speaking out

Small businesses need somebody to look out for them and help them. Bigger businesses can look after themselves, but the people running small firms spend every waking hour simply trying to keep their ventures alive. They are always strapped for money, and there just isn't enough time in the day to do everything. They have nobody to fight their corner either, so when larger companies reduce their customer service, or put their prices up, there is nothing they can do. They just have to take it on the chin. And even if they had the time or the ability to speak out, nobody would listen.

So it is up to somebody like me, who does have a voice, to speak out on their behalf. Over the years, I have been able to speak out on behalf of small businesses on several important issues that make an enormous difference to their ability to survive and thrive. As a business owner, you can't just say you are on the side of small businesses to sell them stuff; you have to genuinely be on their side.

I am passionate about supporting small businesses and the challenges they face because for many years I was running one myself. I know what it is like not to have enough money to pay the bills, or to be working 17-hour shifts for weeks on end and still not having the time to get everything done. So I will not hesitate to fight their corner, whether that is trying to keep the high street alive, curbing excessive business rates, or making it easier for customers to park. Indeed, I feel so strongly about this that I will happily get up at 4am to go on air on the radio and talk about these issues. Small businesses matter to this country and if I can help them, then I will.

I am a strong supporter, for example, of the 'save the high street' campaign. Independent traders are closing down at a devastating rate – according to the Office for National Statistics, around 250,000 UK business close every year. So, it is hugely important to fight for the place where many of them are located, on the high street in every town across the country. The high street is not only the hub of a local economy, but also the heart of every local community. Without it, our vibrant towns and villages will wither and die.

The problem is that high streets are persistently under attack from misguided local and national government policies which unthinkingly deter shoppers from using and enjoying them. I refuse to watch hardworking people and their businesses be ousted from our high streets and will continue to use my voice whenever possible to fight for their survival.

As part of our commitment to the high street, XLN has also supported a campaign calling for free parking on the high street. I feel strongly that expensive parking charges are crippling UK high streets and forcing the small businesses on them to close. Local councils are introducing car-parking charges all the way along high streets, which is having the effect of moving shopping to the bigger, out-of-town stores that are able to offer free parking.

I knew that my voice alone would not be enough to force any kind of change at a national-government level, but I feel that by addressing the issue at a local-government level, it is possible to make something positive happen. So, we created a template letter that small businesses could download from our website and send to their local MP requesting that their council trial free parking on their local high street. It's a simple action to take but the impact it can have is immense. Those councils which have trialled free parking on their high streets have found that it delivers astounding results, encouraging visitors to stay longer and spend more in local shops. It brings the high street back to life and makes an enormous difference to local businesses. We want every high street to be able to experience the benefits of this.

I also feel strongly about encouraging small businesses to take on apprentices and speak out whenever I can about the advantages of doing this. There are considerable benefits to taking on apprentices for small businesses. They improve business productivity, and they are an affordable catalyst for business growth. The government subsidises the training and hiring of apprentices, and even gives businesses a significant incentive fee simply for taking on an apprentice. Apprenticeships can be really beneficial for young people too, giving them practical, on-the-job experience that can be even more useful than academic qualifications.

The problem is that many businesses don't really understand how apprentices work, and so they shy away from taking one on. In fact, XLN did some research which showed that 77% of businesses don't fully understand the laws, processes and details associated with hiring an apprentice. That needs to change.

Here's the bottom line: small businesses make an average profit of £13,000 per year. They simply can't afford to hire anyone else.

Overall, small businesses are essential to a strong economy and I see it as part of my job to champion them and support them in any way I can. In fact, we have come up with five things that could help save small businesses:

1. Teach businesses about the ways they can establish a presence online and why it's important.

2. Show businesses that recruiting is a necessary expense for growth.

3. Make high streets accessible for everyone.

4. Freeze or lower business rates.

5. Help businesses compete with big online retailers by creating communities.

Mentorship

I feel it is also important to give back in other ways. Many people have helped me and mentored me over the years. Nobody gets to my position without somebody looking out for you and helping you along the way. Entrepreneurs are always operating at the edge of their experience and so it is really useful if you can find someone who can mentor you, who has been down the road you are on. That's because they can see the potholes that you can't see, they can tell you which roads are dead ends, or are dangerous, and they can explain to you what your options are. That is so important.

My dad has been crucial in helping me, but there have been many others too. One of them was Henning Deichmann, a very successful Danish entrepreneur and businessman. He helped me a lot in my early formative years. He was a travelling jewellery salesman who pretty much invented plastic jewellery and hair accessories; he built up a big multinational company called Buch and Deichmann. It was hugely successful but grew too quickly and eventually he lost the company. He then started a similar venture called Evita Peroni, which is still very successful worldwide. His experience, mentoring, friendship and wisdom has been invaluable.

Other people who have helped me along the way include Larry Hahn, an entrepreneur who taught me psychology and sales motivation, and Frank McKay, XLN's current chairman. It is so important to learn from the smart people you meet in life. You can discover an enormous amount from them, and it is the quickest shortcut to success – if there ever was one.

I could never have imagined that I would be as successful as I have been, but I made a deal with myself that if I was successful then I would help other people in return. Starting out in business and becoming successful is really difficult; probably 90 out of 100 people fail. So, when I discover young people who I think have what it takes and who are willing to put in the effort, I help them, because what would take months for them to figure out, I can tell them in an hour. The only requirement I have is that they listen to what I have to say and consider it, and if they disagree with it, then we debate it – because I don't want to waste my time, or theirs, for that matter. So far, the young people I have spent time with have exceeded all my expectations.

Ask for help

One thing I have learned and observed in my life is that when I ask for help I usually get it. I'm pretty sure humans have an inbuilt desire to help each other. Likewise, I sadly also think, we are hardwired to believe that asking for help is showing weakness. It is not! Quite the opposite in fact.

It continues to baffle me that some people won't ask for help. Nobody knows everything and anyone who thinks asking for help is a weakness is themselves probably insecure and narrow-minded. I see, again and again, people, employees and colleagues struggle with problems that could easily have been resolved by a collaborative mindset. Don't bury your head in the sand, seek input, ideas and solutions from the people around you. When asking for help, it is advisable to start with, "I really need your help…" or "I'm struggling with … and would love your input".

If asked, I just about always try to help. Helping others makes you feel good.

One of the young people I used to mentor is Ross Gunning, a young conductor who started up the Glasgow Philharmonia youth orchestra. He got in touch with me in 2014, when he was only 19 years old, to ask if I would help and guide him. I really liked Ross and although the orchestra had only done two concerts at that point, he had big dreams for what it could achieve, so I said yes.

Normally, to get into an orchestra you have to have previous orchestra experience, so it is a classic Catch-22 situation. But Ross helps young, aspiring musicians who have studied at school or a conservatoire by enabling them to play in his orchestra and so gain experience that way. I guided him on what he should do and how to do it, and I provided the money he needed to get his vision off the ground. He now puts on 22 concerts a year, playing in concert halls to 2,000 people, and he gets lots of famous West End musical names singing along. It is amazing. His goal is to get his orchestra performing in the Royal Albert Hall.

Another person I help is Tom Oliver, who is my personal fitness trainer. To stop him from ordering me around, we talk about business every morning when I'm on the treadmill. Tom was already successfully creating nutritional products and supplements, but I suggested that he should start making vegan protein bars. He had already had the same idea, so he developed and launched a product which should sell half a million bars in the first year. They are already stocked in about 1,000 pharmacies and outlets in the Middle East. Soon after, I bought 10% of his business because I'm convinced he will be a big success.

I am also helping two Norwegian entrepreneurs who design, produce and sell watches called Brathwait. They currently sell 10,000 watches a year and I advise them on everything from the customer experience to packaging. I ended up buying 20% of their business.

Sometimes bigger opportunities come along too. A great friend of mine who is a very successful investor and entrepreneur, Peter Elbek, told me about a marketing automation business called Agillic A/S. Agillic had developed an amazing technology platform that could do omni-channel marketing automation but had virtually gone bust. We looked at the company and were convinced it was probably the future of marketing. I invested in the business with Peter and in the past couple of years it has achieved an incredible turnaround, recently floating on part of the Danish stock market (Nasdaq First Nordic) for £40m. Right now, we are investing heavily in the eSports and biotech space, as we believe these will be of great interest in the coming years.

These are but a few examples of people and projects I have been involved in, but I'm always open to helping other individuals and investing in exciting opportunities.

One thing that has often been suggested to me is that I should become a non-executive chairman of other companies. At least, once I have retired. My reservations were mainly centred on the thought that once I had retired as CEO, why would I want to be a part-time player in a back-seat-driver type of situation.

How wrong was I?

A head-hunter contacted me and asked if I would like to join a growing Wi-Fi business as chairman. Eventually, after having met the CEO, CFO and private-equity investors, I agreed. The company is called Wifinity and what a journey it has been.

Within a year we managed to refinance the company, buy their biggest competitor, integrate the acquisition, triple profits, and put the company up for sale at four times the value it had when I joined. A life lesson learned yet again: never judge a book by its cover. Say yes to opportunities and see where it leads. That won't be the last time I chair another company.

I also think it is important to give back to my team at XLN. I do this by taking different groups of staff to fun and glamorous events outside the office, both as a reward and as a bonding opportunity. I take three of them to the Monaco Grand Prix every year, for example, and I take small groups of people to events such as Wimbledon, the Queen's Club final, and Henley Regatta. We also tend to go to quite a few high-profile boxing matches, usually at the O2 Arena. In 2019, we had one of these events every single month just for the sales channels.

These events allow me to offer my team once-in-a-lifetime experiences that they would probably never be willing to pay for themselves. It is also an opportunity for us to spend a bit of time together and for me to get to know them on a personal level outside of the office. I think this is really important. As the business grows, that sense of team spirit can often disappear, so I try to bring people together whenever I can, so that everyone feels part of what we are doing.

I also give back to my team by granting them equity in the business, enabling them to share directly in its success. All of my senior managers and around 30 other employees in the company have an equity stake in XLN, which gives them a substantial cheque each time we do a private-equity exit or some other form of liquidity event. I strongly believe in staff equity ownership and encourage all business owners to make key employees fellow shareholders.

If you want your colleagues to feel a sense of ownership about the business, then make them an owner. I so often hear bosses say that they wish their staff would work as hard as them and treat the business as their own. Why on earth should they? They only work there for a salary, which means you rent them for a period of the day. You own the business, and if you want your staff to be fully on board, let them own a piece of it too.

I feel incredibly privileged to still be at the helm – previously as the CEO and now as the executive chairman – of one of the UK's successful businesses, but most importantly, to be surrounded by a team that will also benefit from its success. I could have sold the business long ago, instead of going through all the pain of the past few years, and walked off into the sunset with a ton of money, but for me the victory of making a lot of money would have been very hollow if I was the only one benefiting. I measure my success not by how much wealth I have, but by how much wealth I create for the other shareholders in the business. I am immensely proud that XLN's success has enabled many people working with me to receive life-changing sums of money.

Your company's role in the wider community

You employ people and you pay corporation tax, so in a sense you are making a positive contribution to the wider society you are part of. But I firmly believe it is our responsibility as business leaders to lead by example and try to make the world a better place. Of course, within the limits of what you are capable of.

Over the years, we have supported many charities and youth initiatives, which is a great feeling for both myself and, I believe, the entire XLN team. Two huge issues that are on everyone's agenda and mind are Brexit and climate change.

Brexit has been hugely divisive in our society and as I write, a deal has been signed at last. Whether you were for or against leaving the EU – and I was not in favour – we now find ourselves in the situation where we, as a nation, have left the EU and need to forge a new path. There is no point whatsoever in debating the pros and cons of the decision, as it has already been made. We now need to look to the future, focus on the positives and get on with creating new jobs, businesses and opportunities for a better UK. In every situation there are opportunities, and with the right mindset we can grow and prosper. No point in looking backwards and harping on about what could have been. As Frank McKay would say: "there's no point in looking up a dead horse's ar**."

Climate change is without a doubt one of the biggest challenges that mankind has faced in recent centuries and the way we approach it will determine our species' future on this planet. I believe that all companies can and must try to make a difference.

If we all make little changes in the way we behave and the way we run our businesses, it will add up to make a big, meaningful impact. In this regard, we at XLN have spent part of the lockdown period trying to get our Environmental, Social and Governance (ESG) agenda formulated and implemented.

XLN was one of the first telecoms companies to become carbon neutral back in 2009 and we have now taken the necessary steps towards removing the carbon footprint we have left behind since I founded the company in 2002. In other words, XLN has left no carbon footprint at all since it was formed and will continue that way going forward. I hear many companies proclaiming that by 2030 or 2040 they will be carbon neutral. I realise that some companies have hugely complex operations that cannot be changed overnight, but I still feel that most businesses should be much more ambitious and challenge themselves to get this done in the next few years.

Another initiative we are about to introduce is a partnership with the Rainforest Trust. For every customer that signs up to XLN, we will pay for the preservation of one acre of rainforest. That may not sound like a lot, but over a four-year horizon, we are looking to preserve over 100,000 acres of rainforest, 20m trees and countless species. Every little helps, after all. And this association is in addition to a corporate partnership we already have with Big Blue Ocean Cleanup. We only use recycled paper, plastics and vegetable inks in all our marketing collateral, and continuously look to remove any harmful materials from our supply chain and office use. We will continue to explore all avenues to make a difference and set a good example.

I firmly believe that if you are able to make a positive difference then you owe it to yourself, your colleagues and the wider community – that you are part of – to do so. However big or small.

LIFE LESSON

Find yourself some mentors and listen to them. Always surround yourself with positive people and discard negative ones. And when you can, give something back. You'll find that is the greatest feeling.

PART
TWO

My Core
Principles

Formula For Success

DURING THE 30 years I have been in business, I have come to realise that there are several core principles to the way I run my life and my business which have been fundamental to my success. Some of these principles have been consciously learnt and others have been subconsciously absorbed from the various events that we have been exposed to in our life. We are, in many ways, the sum of our family and friends and the experiences we go through.

In my opinion, all of these principles are absolutely crucial to achieving success in business. They are things that I think about and enact religiously. They are my formula for success, and apply to heavyweight business leaders and budding entrepreneurs alike.

Whether you are running a multinational company or a small business, taking over the world with a new tech start-up or expanding your chain of high-street hairdressers, these are my core principles for winning in business. I hope one or two of them will resonate with you and help you on your journey.

Core Principle 1
Learn Great Work Habits

RIGHT FROM MY earliest days in business, I have always believed in the importance of developing good work habits. In fact, probably the single biggest reason why I am where I am today is because of the work habits I established while I was being trained in field sales in San Francisco.

When I first went out to San Francisco at the age of 22 to learn how to sell perfume, I watched the most successful salespeople at work. Not just how they sold, but how they organised themselves and their days. Eventually, I realised that they all acted in the same way. They worked consistently, and they worked hard – really hard.

They started early, they finished late, and most importantly, they worked with determination, enthusiasm and passion. They sold enormous amounts of perfume, not just every now and then, but regularly and consistently, day after day and week after week. I resolved to model myself and my work habits on them, and for the past 30 years, it has produced amazing results.

The regional manager, Kerry Brunson, who ran San Francisco and the Bay Area, including the office I was assigned to train in, had some of the best office work habits I have ever seen. He was the most organised, hard-working and inspirational leader I have ever met. Many of the habits and traits he showed me, I still use to this day. Kerry became a great friend and came to work with me at XLN in London when we needed to get our field-sales organisation rebuilt and scaled up.

The fact is that if you are going to be successful in life, you need to have great work habits. It is so easy to fritter away your time and not get anything done, but if you want to achieve great things, you need to be disciplined. You have to consciously learn great work habits for yourself and then work to make them stick. They won't just happen by themselves.

And remember, just because you like doing something doesn't make you good at it. That comes through long hours and dedication. All the great artists painted for many years before they were discovered. For example, Peter Morgan, who is probably the best British screenwriter today, having written both *The Crown* and *The Queen* as well as many other world-famous film and theatre scripts, wrote theatre plays throughout school and university and now writes every single day.

Winners are made, not born. To be successful, you need a certain amount of talent or inspiration, but that might only be somewhere between 1% and 10%. The rest is hard work. Mental hard work, emotional hard work and physical hard work.

And remember, these habits should be applied equally to every area of your life – they are meant to be adapted to whatever role you choose to play and every project you find yourself involved in.

Have a great attitude

On average, people are asked the question 'how are you?' 60 times a day. How often do you reply: 'I am unbelievable', 'I am cosmic', 'I am awesome', 'I am so good that if I was any better there'd be two of me'. The answer is never, of course.

We say, 'I'm fine', 'I'm not too bad', 'I'm alright', or even, 'I've been better'. But if you tell yourself 60 times a day that you are 'not too bad', that is lethal – it is absolutely mental suicide. If you tell yourself that kind of rubbish, how the hell can you be confident and believe in yourself? How can you have a fantastic attitude? How can you go out and conquer the world? How can you build a business if you are just 'alright', if you are 'not too bad'?

Your attitude is your mindset, it is the prism through which you view life. If you tell yourself that you are only alright, then you are not going anywhere. You join all the average non-starters and losers in the world. Because they tell themselves day in and day out that they are alright, that they are not too bad.

Do you think Mo Farah thinks he is just alright, that he is not too bad? Do you think you can win a race against the best in the world if you are standing on the starting line thinking, 'I'm not too bad; hopefully I will do alright today'? Do you think that when Sir Alex Ferguson was managing Manchester United, he was saying, 'lads, you are not too bad'? Do you think that is how you become great? It isn't, I can assure you.

What's more, nobody wants to work for somebody who is just alright, who is not too bad. People want to work with and be associated with great leaders who make them better than they would be on their own.

Having a great attitude is not about high fives, group hugs and stuff like that, it is about feeding your brain positive stuff instead of mediocre bull****. If you keep telling yourself that you are average, then you are going to be average. So you need to tell yourself that you are unbelievable, that you are fantastic, that you are awesome, that you have never been better, because if you start putting that sort of stuff into your head a hundred times a day, you will change your mindset.

That's what having a great attitude is all about. It's hard work, but if you keep at it then it will become second nature.

Conscious versus subconscious mind

Just a quick note on the power of your brain and how to use it to your advantage. Which part of your brain do you think is the more powerful: the conscious mind, which is the part you are using right now to absorb the words I've written, or your subconscious mind, which is simultaneously controlling your breathing and heartbeat?

Your subconscious or unconscious mind is roughly 200 times more powerful than your conscious mind. The conscious mind is essentially an underpowered computer with insufficient processing power that's trying to make sense of things as you go through your daily life. Meanwhile, the subconscious mind has almost unlimited, lightning-fast processing power and storage capacity. It controls all your bodily functions – like temperature, blood-sugar level, oxygen level and the like – which are all constantly being adjusted to maintain a level that millions of years of evolution has proved to be optimal.

Conversely, your conscious mind is spending 95% of its capacity reading these words or completing any task it is set to. Hence, it can only focus a maximum of 5% on the environment around you; it simply deletes the rest.

You need to learn to use your subconscious mind to your advantage. While the conscious mind is deleting between 95–97% of what's happening around you, the subconscious mind is recording and storing every single detail, comparing it to past experiences and then updating your internal 'map of the world' for future reference.

In simple terms, the unconscious mind controls every single action you take that you don't have to think about before doing. It is your operating system, so to speak. It creates what are called patterns of behaviour, which allow you to make snap decisions or have instant reactions to situations that have previously been 'mapped out'.

To establish good working habits, you should programme or re-programme your subconscious mind to react in a way that is conducive to your success. This is why I am so passionate about work habits, because I believe that unless you develop great habits and thereby engage your subconscious mind in a way that is aligned with success, you are very unlikely to achieve it consistently or at any great degree.

Be enthusiastic

Enthusiasm is contagious – lack of enthusiasm is contagious too. Positivity is absolutely fundamental to success. If you look back to when you were at school or university, there were some people who were really popular and were always being invited to parties. The reason for that was because they were funny, they were charming, and they were nice to be around.

In the same way, no-one wants to spend ten minutes in the company of someone who is negative because it is draining. Such people have what I call mental BO, and it stinks. Nobody wants to be around it. People like that need to be removed from an office immediately for health and safety reasons. Positivity breeds positivity. Likewise, negativity breeds and attracts negativity. Negativity is like a cancer in a company; you must root it out.

To become successful, you need to be able to get people to follow you, because otherwise they won't want to listen to you and they won't want to buy from you. If you are a manager or a leader, you need people to listen to you and take your advice too, and they are not going to do that unless you are positive and enthusiastic. Human beings are attracted to positivity and confidence, to passion and success, because when we are around people who are enthusiastic and passionate, we feel better.

Such positivity can be expressed in various ways. Enthusiasm is not about shouting and going on endlessly about your products' amazing benefits while you flail your arms around, but more about subtle impulses, such as the way you move, holding eye contact, smiling and your tone of voice. You must learn to control all of these things (there are many great books written on the subject). Your tonality and body language in particular will be recorded by the subconscious mind and will affect the emotional side of your audience.

I am not a naturally enthusiastic person. I wake up in the morning and I am like the Grim Reaper. But I know that when I get to the office, I will have 40 salespeople waiting for me, all of whom will look like death warmed up, and I will need to pump them full of energy. I do this because I know that if I send any members of my team out while they are lacking confidence and have no positivity, then they are dead meat. They won't sell a thing all day, and possibly all week.

So I need to lift them up by being enthusiastic myself. I need to fill them with positive vibes and confidence through stories and material I impart on them. It doesn't matter if you have to fake it a bit; perception is reality and as long as people think you are genuinely enthusiastic, they will be buoyed just the same. But obviously you want to learn the ways and habits of being naturally enthusiastic most of the time, which is achieved by feeding your mind with positive inputs and positive reaffirmations. In its simplest form, keep telling yourself and others that you are great.

Set goals

Setting goals is absolutely fundamental to becoming successful and reaching whatever level you desire. Long-term success is really just an accumulation of many smaller goals that you've reached consistently over a longer period of time. One definition of success, accredited to Paul J Meyer, that I really like is: "Success is the progressive realisation of predetermined, worthwhile, personal goals".

Many great books have been written on how to set, plan and reach your goals. The only thing I will add is this: set big goals. Really big goals.

Having set myself huge goals, I have fallen somewhat short of them most of the time. But because my aspirations were so huge, I was still miles ahead as a result. Don't forget, regardless of whether you aim for Mars or the Moon, the stars or the treetops, the effort is the same. And if you fall short, well, you will be further ahead than you were.

I also find that setting really big goals forces you to think in a different way. You can't reach a huge goal simply by making incremental improvements, or small changes here and there. Big goals require larger-scale improvements; they will take new thinking and a different approach to achieve. It is only after you have taken larger steps that you can start incrementally improving on your operations. Real innovation comes from when the old ways simply won't get you to where you desire to go. Try something big and entirely new – it's super exciting.

I had practically forgotten about this story until now, but it had become almost folklore to the company.

When I started XLN, I was working part-time at Euroffice, the office-supplies internet company I had co-founded a few years earlier. The reason I left to start XLN was because I had realised that Euroffice wouldn't be my ticket to the bigtime. So, the idea came to me that I would start a telephone company (a telco) and build a customer base of 10,000 small companies. We could then flip it, split the money four ways, and at least have something to show for our hard work. Everyone in the industry told me again and again that it was impossible to build a telco that had more than 10,000 customers and £20m in annual revenues/turnover. Hence my goal was seen as being rather unrealistic.

Back in those days, I used to spend two weeks over the Christmas period at an old school friend's farm in Kenya, so I suppose this story must have taken place around December 2002. I usually spent the time relaxing and catching up with Peter Bonde Nielsen and his family. This was in the very early days of the company – we had signed maybe only 500 customers.

All my plans were built around attaining the goal of 10,000 customers and frankly that wasn't proving a trivial pursuit. Peter's camp was built in the Great Rift Valley, at an altitude of 4,000 feet. One evening, I was sitting near the ridge edge as the sun was setting slowly over the magnificent landscape. I had a diet coke in my hand, the sun on my back and was, as always, deeply engrossed in thinking about my business. The goal of 10,000 small-business customers just wasn't sitting well with me.

And then it came to me: 10,000 was the wrong goal. It had to be 100,000 customers!

When I returned to the UK, I sat down with the brothers, my partners in the business, and recounted my story. At this point in time, we had worked together for over four years and they knew full well that when I set myself a goal, I wouldn't be swayed from it. So, we locked ourselves in the conference room until we had found a way of reaching the new goal.

It took a long time, but the way we did it was to start with the goal and then work our way backwards. In essence, if we wanted to have 100,000 customers in the next five years, we needed to sign up around 25–30,000 customers per year, accounting for churn. That's 500–600 live sales per week. We needed 100 sales agents and in order to recruit, train, develop and manage that number, we needed around ten sales offices across the country. So that's exactly what we built over the next two years and we reached something like 750 sales per week. The rest, as they say, is history.

The moral of the story really is that it was just as hard to reach 100,000 as it would have been reaching 10,000, but it was a lot more fun and exciting to aim high. When you have a huge goal, you've got something exciting to communicate and get your troops to rally around. We hit 100,000 customers within six years of my epiphany in Kenya.

Commitment

Now folks, here's the rub. Success cannot be an option. Flip it around, and neither can failure.

So, if you want to be really successful, you need to start setting some big goals and start hitting them with everything you've got. Planning, huge effort and intensity. Long hours and incredible sacrifices. You need to learn to commit and then stick to it.

That's really the hard part. Anyone can dream a big goal and many can plan the way to its attainment, but very few have the cojones to get the bloody job done. So if you want to achieve big things, you need to grow yourself a set of proverbial brass balls and stop crying when the going gets tough.

Success, you must understand, is not something that just happens to you, something that just falls into your lap while you're twiddling your thumbs. It happens because of you and the work you put in. Stop pretending you worked really hard, that life is just unfair, and you were unlucky. These are all excuses. Take responsibility and get on with it. You knew it was going to be hard and let me tell you something, it's only the things we really bust our backsides to obtain that we truly value in the end. Easy comes and all that. So, if you are not prepared to give it everything and never give up, then you might as well put this book down now and try to get a refund.

If you set a goal, give it everything you've got and pursue it until the time is up. If you find you didn't quite hit your goal, then at least you'll sleep well in the knowledge that it wasn't for lack of trying. This habit of giving it your all with total commitment is a crucial part of your development.

Luck

Luck is what losers say they didn't have and successful people say they had a bit of. But anyone that's ever tasted success knows that luck has nothing to do with it. It was sheer hard work, preparation and countless hours of practice honing and developing your work habits.

The harder I work, the luckier I get.

Samuel Goldwyn

The more I practice, the luckier I get.

Gary Player

To some extent, success can seem to have been helped along by luck, but really it is timing that happens to be in your favour. Being in the right place at the right time. But sitting at home feeling sorry for yourself is hardly likely to put you in the right place at the right time either. The only thing that's likely to happen is your partner saying get off your backside and help with some household chores.

To be lucky, and to be in the right place at the right time, you need to be prepared and out there looking for opportunities. And when you happen to be in the right place, you better know what to do with the opportunity. That's where the countless long hours of preparation, lessons learned, and hard work come in. It's so that you are ready when your big break comes.

Excuseitis

This is a term we coined in San Francisco; it refers to a disease of the mind that befalls most people that won't take responsibility for their actions and often their lack of effort. If you want to make it big, you have to be honest with yourself and stop blaming God and sundry for your poor results. Sometimes the cookie crumbles in a way that means you don't quite get the results you deserved, but likewise, sometimes you get a bit more. Over the longer term, this always averages out.

It's OK to realise that you just didn't give it your all today, but you mustn't let that become a habit.

Making excuses for not delivering is the root of all mediocrity and a sure way to become a gilt-edged loser. I can't begin to tell you the number of excuses I've heard in my time, but the reality is that you either deliver, or you don't. As my first sales manager used to say:

"production talks and bull**** walks". Similarly, Frank McKay, XLN's current chairman, would always say: "the excuse shop is closed".

Here are some of the excuses I have heard: the territory had been worked already; I didn't have the right products; customers just didn't want to buy; it was too cold, too hot, too wet, etc. I've even heard things like: My uncle died; my goldfish drowned; my girlfriend doesn't want me to work late; I didn't have money for the bus; I got lost; everyone I saw had already bought; and so on and on and on. And my absolute favourite: my hand got stuck in the cornflake pack.

There seems to be no end to the inventiveness and number of excuses losers can come up with. The upshot of the saga is that they just won't take responsibility and be accountable for their own actions; it is always someone else's fault that they didn't succeed. That's bull****. If you fall into that trap of the mind, you will never be successful. True, bad things happen and stuff gets in the way, but that's life. The trick is to overcome those obstacles and move forwards.

You must learn how to overcome obstacles, as there will always come a time – in any journey towards whatever goal you have set – where the going gets tough and you'll feel like quitting. Just remember, winners never quit and quitters never win.

Be prepared. Plan and visualise

Know what is ahead of you. When I was working in field sales, I would carefully plan my territory and my tactics in advance. On Sundays, I would look at the area I was going to cover the next week and decide where I was going to start and where I was going to end. To mentally prepare myself, I would try to visualise the customers I was going to meet.

I would also have my paperwork and samples prepared and packed. I would choose what I was wearing the night before so that I didn't have to think about it in the morning. You shouldn't be scrambling around in the morning because the shirt you wanted to wear hasn't been ironed and your shoes aren't polished, or spending all your time commuting to work trying to get your head on straight. You don't need that. You need to focus on getting psyched up.

This obviously applies in all areas. I may not go into the field selling perfume anymore, but I do meet bankers, private-equity directors and other high level businesspeople from within and outside of my industry. If I have an important meeting lined up, I will mentally visualise who will be in the meeting, the topics we need to cover and the likely tricky questions I'll be asked. That way, I'm not taken by surprise when a question pops up and I'm not intimidated by the setting, attendees or occasion.

Be rigorous

There is a method to working properly. If you work in the field, you have to work all the back streets, side streets and first-floor offices, as well as the main streets and big offices, because that is where most of the sales actually come from. You should never skip a door, be it internal or external. It's the same when you are making calls; you have got to have a high contact rate, because the sales will always come from the people you least expect. Go about your work in a methodical and organised fashion, and never judge a book by its cover. Deal with every person in the same way and put the effort in with everyone.

The same applies in all other aspects of your business. If you are raising funds, keep going and keep looking for new investors – you never know who is going to invest. If you are looking for a new employee or supplier, or looking for ways to solve a problem that is impeding your business performance, keep going. Never leave any stone unturned.

Executivitis - Not working hard enough

If you are not prepared to work 12–18 hours a day, six or seven days a week, then you are not going to achieve much or become a big success. It is that simple. And you have to work with intensity. It is no good having breaks all the time. The equation to remember is:

$$\text{Hours} \times \text{Intensity} \times \text{Ability} = \text{Results}$$

You have got to put the hours in, but simply sitting at your desk isn't going to achieve anything; you need to work with intensity too. If one person calls 30 potential customers an hour for ten hours, they will be speaking to 300 people. Whereas, if someone else calls 15 potential customers an hour for six hours, they will only speak to 90 people. That's a factor of 3.3. It's no wonder that the first salesperson will do better and go further, assuming similar abilities.

That has been my philosophy in life – put the hours in and work with an intensity that is unreal. Make it a habit. This is hard to do in the beginning, but if you stick at it, you will end up putting four times as much effort in over a lifetime, meaning you will be eight times further along the road.

If you put the effort in, you will achieve success. It is that simple. I can't tell you whether it is going to be in three months, three years or 30 years, but I can tell you it is going to happen. The level of intensity and hard work is pretty unreal though. Hence, it is absolutely imperative that you enjoy what you do. Can you imagine having to work from 7am to 9pm Monday through Sunday if you hated what you were doing? It would be unbearable and frankly not sustainable in the long run. I have always gone to bed exhausted but looking forward to getting out of bed again the next morning. Loving what you do, that's heaven – you will never have to work another day in your life.

One of my first mentors used to tell me: "Christian, hard work comes in three stages. First, you work hard; then, you work harder;

finally, you bust your arse." When I started my career as a lowly sales agent in San Francisco, I learnt to work long hours. As an agent, you only have 24 hours in a day; you do need to eat and sleep too, so there's a natural limit on how much you can achieve.

Once you progress to management, and essentially multiply your efforts through the people you manage, it only makes sense, at least to me, to increase your input. So, you should be working even harder with increased intensity and efficiency. Finally, once you reach the stage of leadership, it's time to really bust it. If, like me, you have an organisation of 500 people, every hour of effort you put in is multiplied by 500. So why wouldn't you give it your all? You can literally achieve a year's worth of results by lunch time.

I love this saying: it is not what you can do that matters, but what you can do through others that really counts.

The problem I see time and again is that as soon as an agent starts getting good at selling, they begin to work less and their results plateau. How many times have you noticed a new recruit's output drop after they begin to hit their targets? How is it possible that their results remain constant as their skill and ability improves with increased experience?

Well, the answer is simple; they start getting lazy and start developing poor work habits. It is sadly human nature to become lazy, but it is your job as their manager to resist that and encourage a consistent level of input so that your employee's paycheque increases with their increased level of skill and experience. If you allow poor work habits to develop, the following will inevitably happen; their production will take a dive, their attitude will deteriorate and eventually they will quit the job, blaming you and the company. What a waste.

And that's not the worst that can happen! What's more likely to be the case is that the agent would have started to work with other new recruits, in either a training or managerial role. Now their bad habits and poor attitude are being transposed onto otherwise promising agents, and your organisation will start to slowly rot from within.

Sorry to harp on about this subject, but I simply cannot stress strongly enough just how much effort is needed to be applied consistently over a very long period. There is no such thing as an overnight success. The reason it seems like it happened overnight is that you weren't privy to all the preparation and the insane amount of intense work that has gone into getting to the point where success becomes visible to the bystander.

One of the mistakes I see people make is that they underestimate the effort that is required when they start planning how to reach a particular goal. Over the years, I have seen hundreds of business plans and met the entrepreneurs and management teams behind those plans. I have yet to see a business plan that I think is remotely realistic. At the very least, they always overestimate projected sales by a factor of two, and underestimate the cost and time it takes by a factor of two. Often, it's much worse than that, but that isn't really the fatal mistake.

The killer is that the effort required is so vastly underestimated that they risk giving up long before they even get close to building something profitable. As long as you genuinely understand the effort required and have prepared for that, then you stand a pretty good chance. That is why most venture capitalists prefer to back a founder or team that has failed a number of times. The assumption is that they learned some hard lessons along the way.

In the same way, venture capitalists prefer to back a great management team with an average idea over an average team with a fantastic idea. The great team will change the idea if necessary, whereas the average team is likely to screw up the amazing idea or quit because the going gets too tough.

Don't set limits

At XLN, we have the lowest rate of churn in the telecoms industry, which means that we have the lowest proportion of customers who leave us for a competitor. Now, a lot of people in my position might say, well, we are doing better than everyone else in our industry, so we must be doing something right. We can sit back, relax and focus on something else. But I don't think like that.

Just because we are already the best, doesn't mean we aren't able to do better. Don't simply compare yourself and your business to your competitors. Focus on what you would like your business to be in an ideal world and continuously work towards that by improving every aspect of your operation. Never compare yourself to others, only compete with yourself. There will always be people richer than you, and people worse off than you. If you compare yourself, you will either feel superior or inferior. That makes for a pretty emotionally screwed up life.

I call this approach 'continuous incremental improvement'. It is about always seeking to improve what you are doing. A word of warning here: where you spend your time is critical. Don't get sucked into re-arranging the reception furniture, spend your time wisely. Focus on the areas that make the biggest difference to your business.

Forget about your work-life balance

Now that I have reached the level I have, I can afford to have a good work-life balance. I can go home in time to pick my son up from school occasionally, I can spend the evening playing with him, and I can go out for dinner with my wife and friends. But when you are just starting out in business, you don't have this luxury. You don't have the resources – the money, the people, etc. – and you can't afford them anyway, so you have to do everything yourself. And that means you have to make sacrifices.

At the beginning, you will have to work 12- to 18-hour days, six or seven days a week, with no holidays except the odd long weekend. You will miss out on seeing your partner and you will miss out on seeing your children. That's simply how it is; there is no way around this. You have got to work all the hours, all the time, and even when you are not working, you still need to be thinking about it. You can never take your tie off, because otherwise you cannot and will not build a successful business. Until very recently, my work-life balance was probably 90–10; today, it is more like 80–20.

Save money

This is really important: saving money is one of the best habits you can develop.

My dad always drummed into me that you must never, ever spend more than you earn. Even if it is only by a few pounds a month. It matters. My old boss used to say that there is only one thing worse than being broke, and that is being old and broke. Living beyond your means is a way to guarantee misery.

When I was running a commission-only sales teams, I would force my guys to save money every week. As a result, a funny thing happened; once they had a few hundred pounds saved up, they would start to get greedy – in a good way – and take pride in the amount they saved each week. As I always told them: "It's not how much money you make that matters but how much you save that really counts". Suddenly, they each had £500 in their bank account that they didn't want to touch. After that, they became obsessed with reaching £1,000 and so on. It is a fact that once you have money in the bank, you become a different person – a better one, for that matter.

Core Principle 2
Always Be On

I T SEEMS TO be common practice for some people in business to set aside windows of time on particular days to deal with certain tasks, like coming up with a new product or thinking about strategy. They then just hope that magic will happen in that short, designated time slot.

But to my mind, that's a crazy way of going about things. Ideas and strategies are not going to pop into your head on a certain day at a certain time just because you have set time aside and have decided that they should.

It's far better to be constantly thinking about your business so that you are receptive to the moment that lightning strikes. I usually go to bed every night buzzing with ideas, thinking, 'great, let's sleep now because I can't wait to get out of bed tomorrow and work on this'.

It's a good idea to have a little notebook by your bed, just in case you get a great idea. Always write stuff down. As my dear friend Billy Reynolds (RIP) used to say: a short pencil is better than a long memory.

Always be open to new thoughts and ideas

Having new ideas is not something I can pencil in for a particular time in the week. I need to be constantly coming up with new thoughts and angles. Telecoms is the most competitive commodity industry in Europe and I am fighting BT, Vodafone, Sky, TalkTalk and Virgin Media, all of whom are multi-billion-pound companies. If I am not on my toes, if I am not constantly moving and evolving, then I am a dead duck.

I am constantly on the lookout for new ideas that will improve our operations and make a difference in every area of the business. I am always thinking about how we can come up with something that sets us apart – whether that's in customer service, products or pricing. If there is something that I want to find a solution to, or some department I want to have a different focus, then I will fill my head with what competitors and other successful companies are doing in order to consider what we could be doing and what is possible. I will actively try and seek out as much relevant information as I can from all the places I can think of. Then I know that eventually a good idea will crystallise and drop into my lap.

You need to immerse yourself in the subject and focus on it; think about what is possible, what would be good and what would be ideal. If you have all that good stuff swirling around in your mind, then when you are in the shower, playing golf, or walking the dog, a brilliant idea is going to materialise. By immersing yourself in a subject like this, your subconscious will continually file and organise the material until, as if by magic, an idea will pop out. This will often happen when you least expect it – hence, the notepad at the ready.

Remember that ideas can come from anywhere

It is a mistake and a fallacy to think that good ideas come from more senior or experienced people. Likewise, you don't have a monopoly on great ideas. In actual fact, some of the best ideas often come from new or inexperienced people that see things differently, who aren't shackled by industry or group thinking and can think beyond 'because this is how we've always done it' or 'this is how we did it in my old job/company'. This is another reason why apprenticeships can be so valuable to a business.

Throughout my career, I've always used my dad as a sounding board, particularly when I've faced tricky situations. His usual response has always been, "Christian, I'm old and don't understand your business, but why don't you think about it like this?" or, "have you considered doing it this way?" Very often, we get stuck in the weeds and can't see the wood for the trees. It is therefore incredibly helpful to have someone with no preconceived notions, someone positioned way up in the helicopter, offer a fresh perspective. Inevitably, my dad's input has always been spot on, so clear and simple. Real-life experience from a long career in business, no matter the area, is invaluable, so use it if you've got access to it.

Keep your eyes open for opportunities

As businesses grow, they often tend to close their eyes to new opportunities because they have so many other things going on that take up their attention. Some business owners also get lazy and complacent – it is much easier to watch the money flowing in from existing ventures than look for new projects to take on and develop.

But if you are going to build a successful business, you need to stay alert all the time, constantly looking beyond the current business for new opportunities. Attend conferences, get networking and go to industry dinners. You never know who you might end up sitting next to – they might just turn out to be interesting and potentially useful for your business. You may even meet someone with the potential to become an investor, board member, mentor or employee.

Regardless of how boring the person sitting next to you at the dinner is, or how dull the conference or seminar is, I can practically guarantee that I will walk away with at least one idea that I can apply to my business, and I may even go away with a bucket load of ideas. That's why it is so important to say yes to the invitations and get out there. In the interest of full disclosure, I don't particularly enjoy these kinds of events and have too often shied away from them, but when I look back, I have inherently always come away with something useful. Alas, I hereby resolve to attend more of those events in the future.

Keep your office door open

I get tons of requests from people to come and meet me for a chat. If it sounds interesting, I will say, "yes, come by and have a cup of coffee". It will take 30–45 minutes out of my day and it may turn out to be a waste of time, but it also might turn out to be useful in some way. I'm open to doing this because I know that I don't have the monopoly on good ideas or good practical advice. If I want to learn and move on, I've got to make time for these chats and you should as well.

Don't try to do everything at the same time

Being always on is a brilliant way to create a successful business, but my employees do not always agree with me. I've learnt that it can cause chaos to the people around you if you are constantly bombarding them with new ideas. So, you need to be always on, but you also need to learn how to manage that.

I am constantly coming up with new ideas and I used to tell my team, we should do this, we should do that. But that simply meant that everyone would get overwhelmed and confused. They would be asking each other, are we working on this? Or that? No-one had a clue what to prioritise and what to put to one side.

We would end up with a situation where my team would be wondering about the 40 or so ideas I had come up with – 'is Christian really keen on those? Where do they go on the priority list?' Then everyone would be thinking, 'Christian wants this to happen; so does that mean the project I'm working on should be put to one side? Or what?' I would always want everything to be done as quickly as possible too, which would make things worse. Some of my people have literally spent years in a state of constant confusion because 'ah, Christian had another idea.'

In a business, you've got limited time and resources. My policy is now to ask: what are the three things we are going to work on? Then let's work on those, and let's do it right. And then let's move onto the next three things on the priority list. This was a hard lesson to learn and I only just learnt it recently, with stern guidance from Neil Pirie.

Focus on your strengths

Opinions differ on this subject, but I am 100% convinced that you should focus on your strengths. We all have strengths and weaknesses, and areas that we like more than others. Some people spend a lot of energy, time and effort trying to improve the areas they are not so good at. I don't believe in that. If you are weak in an area that you don't enjoy, then I bet you will never get that good at it. The fact is, you will never be brilliant at everything.

So make a choice: would you rather be brilliant in the areas where you already have talent and that you really enjoy, or work on a weakness that you hate?

My philosophy is that you double down on the areas where you are brilliant and get even better at them. So good, in fact, that only you can do the job. And then you hire or surround yourself with people that have the skills you lack. At least, that's what I do.

When I was a kid, my brother and I would sit outside in the sun with a magnifying glass and burn holes in pieces of paper. If I'm honest, I think some ants lost their lives too. If you hold a magnifying glass still for long enough, the paper will burn; but if you keep moving it around, it won't catch fire. And it is the same with business. You have got to concentrate on the areas where you are the best – where nobody else can do what you can do – and then focus for a period of time. Just like holding the magnifying glass still so that the paper can burn. In business, you need to hire people for all the stuff you can't do, don't like doing or aren't good at.

As I might have mentioned, I wasn't that academic in school; I was what you might call a C-student. But my dad always told me not to worry too much about that. He would say, "Christian, let me tell you. In life, the A and B students always end up working for the C students". And he was right, they all became lawyers, bankers, consultants and accountants – and I rent them by the hour.

Always focus on your strengths. The things only you can do. The things you enjoy and are the best at. Then, support yourself by hiring brilliant people that can supplement you in the areas you are not good at and don't enjoy.

Core Principle 3
Be Accountable

I BELIEVE THAT THE fish stinks from the head down. If something isn't working in a business, the rot starts at the top. The stink is caused by the direction or the behaviour of the person who is in charge. And at XLN, that ultimately means me. So, if the business stinks, I'm the reason. It's my fault. I need to own the problem, and sort it out.

When you are running a company, you have to take full and total accountability for what is going on in it. Forget about the idea of delegating and stepping back to let others take the blame. That's not my style. If there is something going wrong, whether it is to do with the products, the service, the culture, or the organisation of the business, it is my responsibility to fix it. The buck stops with me.

Creating a successful business is not about dreaming about which fast car or yacht you are going to buy next. It is about being completely hands on and being prepared to get totally stuck in and sort out the problems. You need to focus on the minutiae to stop problems escalating. And you need to do it all the time.

This is how I put it into practice in my life.

Remember where you come from

When you start a business, all you really have is a dream and a vision. There is very little to show for what you hope to create. You only have a few people working with you and everyone has to get involved with building the business – in my case, even to the extent of building their own desks to save money. So, you really have to get these people to believe in you and trust you.

When your people agree to work for you, you are basically making a deal with them that says, 'look, this is my vision, this is what we are going to build. I need you guys to believe in me and trust that we are going to succeed'. Often you can't pay them large amounts of money, so you offer them equity in the business instead, which at that point is worth precisely nothing. The people who joined XLN in the early days took a chance on me and were willing to go into battle with me. I therefore feel that it is my responsibility not only to make sure that the business succeeds, but that these individuals become successful too. I have to repay their trust and faith in me.

Know your business inside out

Every month, around a hundred key performance indicators (KPIs) are presented to me by the managers of each department within XLN; they show how the business has been performing over the past month and against the last three months. I look at those numbers and, because I know the business inside out, I can see straightaway if something doesn't look right or if we are not performing at the level that I think we should be.

We call these operational-review, or ops, meetings and they happen every month, religiously. It was one of the things I learned from Frank McKay, XLN's current chairman. Frank had spent a lifetime working for American conglomerates. Before retiring, he was chief executive of Travis Perkins, the builders' merchant, and under his leadership, the company grew from £650m in sales to £3bn.

But Frank's retirement didn't last that long. Clayton, Dubilier & Rice (CD&R), a very large American private-equity firm, had bought a catering company called Brakes Bros Ltd (now just Brakes) for £750m and after five years, the value hadn't increased. They were in trouble. So, CD&R managed to convince Frank to help them out as CEO. Within three years, Frank had turned the business around and sold it for £1.4bn to Bain Capital. Boom. Frank is the best operator I have ever met and I'm very fortunate to have him both as chairman of our board and as my mentor.

Ops meetings were one of the very first things I implemented, with the help and direction of Frank, after the GSO deal was concluded. We have now been running them for 5–6 years and it has transformed the business in some respects. First, it allows us to run very fast while also keeping a close eye on the details. Second, having my key-department managers, all 20 or 30 of them, sit together and examine each other's KPIs has given everyone a much better understanding of the business as a whole and what makes it work. They have also fostered cross-departmental collaboration, as these meetings are as much about helping each other with ideas and working together as they are about anything else. Finally, ops meetings allow me to direct the troops towards problem areas quickly and decisively.

A word of warning here: don't be discouraged if your first five or six ops meetings are a complete shambles. It takes time for every manager to get used to living by their new KPIs. We initially spent a fair amount of time deciding on the three or four KPIs that would best tell the story of each department. Then we needed to get every manager to focus on and live by those KPIs. Perseverance and sticking to your guns are key here. Each meeting does get easier though, and soon the entire organisation will be joined in a common terminology, focus and direction. It's about constant incremental improvement, not perfection.

When I am in the office, I am either having chats with people to see if their area is running as expected and if there's anything I can help with, or I'm poking into everything I can get my hands on to see whether I can make a department run more efficiently. I shine a bright light into every dark corner of the business, using my nose to guide me. I can sense when something doesn't look right or when something smells wrong. So I sniff and scratch a bit and say, yes, there is something here. And then I will go straight from the overview right into the detail, right into the septic tank, to find out what exactly is going on. I never want to miss anything and so far, I rarely have. I'm not trying to catch anyone out, we are all on the same side, but I have a lot of experience and intuitive understanding of where the issues lie. I genuinely just want to help my team get better and succeed in their departments.

Get hands on

What basic, repeated action lies at the very heart of your business?

At XLN, it's looking after our customers. This usually involves making phone calls to prospective customers, serving existing customers and speaking to customers who are thinking of leaving. That is what we do, hundreds of times an hour, every hour, day in, day out. So, we need to make sure that they are good calls and that they achieve what they set out to do every single time.

One day, I realised that I was not seeing the results that I expected from our retention calls (calls to customers who are thinking of leaving us). We should be retaining 70% or 80% of customers who want to leave us, but we were only saving 50%. So I asked one of my sales managers to give me ten random calls to listen to.

Now, listening to calls is about as basic as it gets if you are the CEO of a business, but this is the approach I have always taken. It is no good just listening to what your managers are telling you, because they are likely to tell you what they think you want to hear or what they have been told. You have to take the temperature yourself. It is also a great way of leading by example because if your managers see that the CEO is listening to sales calls, they will realise that maybe it is a good idea if they do too.

On this occasion, when I listened to the sample, I immediately realised that we had people making phone calls who shouldn't be making phone calls at all because they didn't have the right kind of voices for telesales. Either they didn't speak English well enough for people to understand them, or the tone they adopted wasn't appropriate. We had people who were talking to clients like they were their mate from the 'hood' and it was totally unacceptable. 'Innit' is not a word I ever want to hear.

There was no structure to the calls, their knowledge of what our competitors were offering wasn't good enough, and their passion and listening skills simply weren't there either. I was furious – but I was also excited, because improving the quality of those calls was such an easy fix that could quickly deliver a real boost to the entire business.

Make it your responsibility to sort out the problem

Whenever I discover something that is not working properly in my business, I always start with the assumption that as the manager in charge hasn't already fixed it, it is because I haven't taught them well enough. Perhaps it is that they simply don't know any better. It is my responsibility to teach them how they can fix the problem, so that in the future, they can do it themselves.

In the case of the poor retention phone calls, I immediately introduced a training programme that taught managers how to start hiring better people for their sales teams and then how to train them better to make good phone calls. If you are in the service business, you have got to be able to give 'great phone'.

I used to run training calls myself twice a week for anyone in the business who needed it, and I will go into the office on Saturdays to teach people if that's what it takes. Ultimately, the responsibility for getting it right lies with me. Culture is the DNA of your company and it starts at the top. Nobody can express better than you what you want your business to be.

If a manager is still not able to fix the problem even after I have trained them, then they will have to leave the business. They are clearly part of the problem, and I have a responsibility to the other people in the business to get it right. After all, if someone is not part of your solution to success, then they are part of the problem.

Success starts at the bottom

If I want to be successful, I have to make sure that the person at the bottom of the pyramid is successful. I have to be accountable for their success. Because if they don't succeed, then the managers and team leaders above won't succeed, and so the company won't be successful. It's simple: if the company doesn't succeed, I don't succeed.

Whenever anyone joins XLN, I make a deal with them. If they are willing to put in long hours and work hard with intensity, then it is my responsibility to make them successful. I have to give them a great product to sell; I have to provide them with a framework and an environment that is conducive for success; I have to teach them product knowledge, a good pitch and work habits; and I have to motivate, inspire and develop them mentally so that they can progress and be successful, no matter what department they happen to be in.

If what I tell them doesn't translate into the right results, such as promotion and a bigger pay packet, then that is ultimately my fault, because I have made a pledge to them. If a department is not moving forward and everyone's careers have stalled, then I will have utterly failed.

Talk to your customers

If you want to know what your business could be doing better, for example, what other products or services you should be selling, how you could improve your pricing, or how you could provide better customer service, go out and speak to your customers. And I do mean YOU, personally. They will tell you the answers you seek. You don't need to hire an expensive consultant, you don't need to create a bunch of reports, and you don't need to delegate the task to anyone else. You just need to go out, visit ten customers yourself and spend a day talking to them.

That's what I do and it provides amazing insights into the business – and all of it for free. I am always speaking to customers on the phone, responding to their emails and going to visit them in their shops and businesses in their local community. Don't hide yourself away in an office. You will find out so much more this way. When your employees see that you are fanatical about your customers' well-being and the service you provide, that will soon enough permeate throughout your organisation.

Core Principle 4
Just Make The Bloody Decision

WHEN YOU ARE an entrepreneur, you will have to make a lot of decisions. And, regardless of how smart you happen to be, you will almost always be operating at the edge of your experience and your comfort zone. Hence, when you're faced with a new problem, you will often only have a 50/50 chance of being right. In other words, some things you will get right and some things you will get wrong. That can be hard.

But the most important thing is not whether you make the right or wrong decision – the most important thing is that you actually make a decision. I once had a chief operating officer who I had to fire after nine months because the person was incapable of making a decision until they were 100% sure that it was the right one. I had a business partner who was the same. He would take ages to make a decision because he had to gather all the information first. We used to joke that he would fill a bathtub with all the information and then just lie in it for a week.

We are all different, but I tend to make decisions immediately. That doesn't mean I don't consider the available information or listen to other people, or indeed contemplate the known unknowns – I just do it quickly. Some decisions turn out to be wrong and others right, but regardless, they are made quickly. At least if they are wrong, they can be corrected quickly.

Indecisiveness kills an organisation because everyone is in limbo while they wait on a decision. Here are some things that I find ease the decision-making process.

Know where you are heading

If you have a clear vision of where you are going and the route you are taking to get there, then it makes decision making much easier. Just ask yourself: does this decision fit the direction we are going in and does it tally with my values and what I believe in?

The clearer and brighter the beacon of your vision, the easier it is to make good decisions. Of course, experience plays a huge role in good decision making. That's why I keep harping on about surrounding yourself with experienced businesspeople who have made some of these mistakes before.

Remember that wrong decisions can be fixed

You will find out fairly quickly whether a decision was the right or wrong one. The good thing with making the wrong decision is that you can correct it – the added bonus being that now you have gained a bit of experience that you can draw on later when you are faced with something similar. So, if it is the right decision, great, and if it is the wrong one, have the humility to say, 'hold on, I made a mistake here. Sorry about that, now we are doing it this way instead'.

Sometimes, decisions – even good ones – have unintended and unforeseen consequences that may not manifest themselves for a period of time. Of course, you should give thought to potential consequences of any decision you're about to make, but the nature of unintended and unforeseen consequences is that they kick you in the backside when you least expect it. Only experience can prepare you and teach you how to reduce the frequency and severity of unintended consequences. I see this most often from inexperienced politicians and arrogant business leaders.

If, like in the former's case, you have very little or no practical experience at all, you inevitably can't calculate what knock-on effects your decisions might have. I have often thought that a certain amount of real-life experience should be a requirement for all politicians. Or that there should be a certain quota of businesspeople in any government. Sadly, we seem to have created a political environment where it is so unattractive for experienced people to get involved that we have a political system governed by the lowest common denominator. An idiotocracy, rather than a meritocracy.

The latter category, of arrogant business leaders, suffers from a know-it-all attitude and is unwilling to listen to other viewpoints as they seemingly think it's a show of weakness not knowing everything. These leaders quickly alienate great employees and steer their companies into decline and oblivion.

Meritocracy

I have always been a proponent of meritocracy. I grew up in Denmark in the 70s and 80s and I can honestly say that I had no idea what religion or otherwise my classmates and family friends belonged to. It simply wasn't something that had any merit in our society back then. I shared a room at boarding school with a good friend whose surname was Goldberg and it wasn't until I had lived in the UK for some time that it dawned on me that he might have been Jewish. That sort of thing is simply not important in business and shouldn't be in any other part of life.

When recruiting salespeople back in the day, I would often say, "I don't care whether you have a double-barrelled surname, a first-class degree from Oxbridge, or are white, black, blue, yellow or polka dotted. I don't care whether you are Muslim, Christian, Jewish or otherwise. The only thing I care about is that you are able to do the job. If you can do the job, you should have the job".

I realise that this is a very sensitive and emotionally-charged subject nowadays, one that most middle-aged, white business leaders – like me – steer well clear of, especially as the pitfalls and potential consequences of such a discussion can be horrendous. Inequality and racism is not lost on me and I abhor all forms of it, but any form of discrimination based on anything but merit seems to me to be entirely stupid and counterproductive in business and society in general. I fail to understand why a business leader would not promote or hire a capable individual just because of some external criteria. That's just bad business.

The only criteria that should be considered is whether an individual is suitable and capable of doing a job as well as or better than any other candidate. Likewise, I can't see it being in the interest of any business to promote an individual to a position they are not suited for just because it ticks some arbitrary minority-inclusion box.

For the avoidance of any doubt, my firm belief is that merit is the only correct criteria for selection. I also believe that a varied and inclusive workforce is much better than a homogenous one.

Trust your gut instinct

One of the things I have learnt over the years is to trust my gut instinct more than my intellectual instinct. If it feels wrong, don't do it. This is particularly true when it comes to hiring people. If it isn't working out and doesn't feel right, then it is probably not going to feel any better six months or a year down the road.

Gut instinct is essentially your subconscious letting you know that, based on all the observations and stored experience of the past, what you are contemplating is not lining up properly. You should listen very carefully to that feeling.

Accept that you can't know everything

No matter what decision you are trying to make, you will never have all of the information. I would say that rather than aiming for 100%, you should try to gather maybe 70–75%. If you see a shadow of a duck on the wall and you hear something quacking, you should go with the assumption that there is a duck somewhere close. The COO I hired would have needed to know the gender and species, as well as collect the DNA of the duck in question before being prepared to make a decision about whether there was a duck over there or not.

Treat every mistake as school fees

If you get a decision wrong and it costs you money to put right, just look at it as school fees – in other words, you have just paid for an invaluable lesson that taught you a huge amount. A bit like paying for a training course, only quicker, more intense and possibly a bit more brutal. You learn much more from your failures than you ever do from your successes, so just accept that this time you paid to be taught a lot of knowledge that might come in handy one day.

Core Principle 5
Forget About Perfect

EVERY ENTREPRENEUR WANTS to be perfect. It's who we are; it's in our DNA, just like being a control freak is. But of course, perfect doesn't exist, so that's madness. You have to fight the urge to be perfect and become pragmatic instead. It is the only way you will get to where you want to be.

Go early

When you are launching a new product or service, it is tempting to think that you should wait until you have perfected it. But that is precisely the wrong thing to do. The right thing to do is to launch it as soon as it reaches a point where you are able to launch it, and then refine it from that point onwards. At XLN, we call this the minimal viable product (MVP) and it's a generally accepted term in business. This means that a product has been built to the minimum possible point that will enable it to be launched.

Study the feedback

Take, for example, an email that you want to send out to your customers. You have no idea how your audience is going to respond to it, so the first version should simply say what you want it to. The key is to then analyse the data that comes back, which will show you how many people opened it, how many people read it, how long they spent reading it, which part of the email they read and which part they didn't. You can measure this with heat-mapping software that is generally available.

Based on the information returned, you then change the variables – what's in the subject line, what day and time of day you send it out – and send it out again to a different group of people. Then, when you get the data back, you tweak and send it out once more. Keep doing that until you get the best possible level of customer engagement.

This is the principle of continuous incremental improvement, which I use in everything I do. In this case, we start with the minimal viable product and improve it using data we receive back from customers until we get it right.

What you want may not be what they want

One of the classic mistakes everyone makes is to say that because I like the colour blue, everybody else should like the colour blue. Or, because I think this reads well, everyone should like it. If you think that you can get the email perfect before you send it, you are delusional – you don't know what people want. Your customers will always show you what works and what doesn't, you can't intellectualise that process.

Core Principle 6
Surround Yourself
With A-Players

GREAT COMPANIES ARE built on great people. While I was at business school, there was great discussion among business leaders and educators – like Jack Welch, Tom Peters, Robert H Waterman and Peter Drucker – about the best kind of people to employ. Over the years, I have adapted my own version of Jack Welch's philosophy, that the people you want to surround yourself with, both in business and in life, are what he calls the 'A-Players'.

A-players are usually easy to identify because they are the people who share the values of your business and can deliver a high performance.

It would be remiss of me not to mention my trusted right-hand man, Tony Fitzpatrick, who helped me through the early Euroffice days and most of the difficult growing pains at XLN. While we were starting Euroffice, in a serviced office building near Putney Bridge, Tony was one of the very first employees I hired. He was fairly young and had worked for Estée Lauder in customer service. We couldn't afford to pay high salaries, so Tony started on something like £22,000 a year, but we gave him equity in the business. Tony was very personable and an amazing guy with the ability to find a solution to just about any operational problem. We built the service and operational side of Euroffice, which says quite a lot. There wasn't any problem we couldn't solve together.

When I left Euroffice to start XLN, Tony stayed behind. Fairly soon after, it became clear to me that I needed his help, expertise and counsel if I wanted to succeed in building all the customer-facing functions. I convinced Tony to jump ship and leave behind all the equity he was due at Euroffice and come build XLN with me. Over the next ten years, we went through hell together but never once did he let me down. I can honestly say that XLN would not be the company it is today without his involvement. I will always have amazing and fond memories of all the trials and tribulations we faced and overcame together.

Almost 15 years at my side, building two companies, takes its toll and Tony eventually decided to retire and live a less hectic life. He left a millionaire and is now happily managing a growing property portfolio. I think of him often and miss him dearly. If, or when, you find a diamond like Tony, never ever let them go. You can't do it on your own.

Values come ready formed

The kind of values you have as an adult are pretty much the values that your parents instilled in you as you were growing up. The values that I grew up with, for example, included work hard, watch the pennies, don't be frivolous or arrogant, and if you are going to do something, then do it really well the first-time round.

By the time you reach the age of 16, your values are pretty much set in stone, which means that as an employer, you can't hope to begin instilling new or different workplace values. Instead, you need to look for people who already have the right kind of values that you need, such as a positive, open mind; a can-do attitude; enthusiasm and passion; honesty; a willingness to work hard; and discipline.

These A-players are the people you need to build your business around. You should promote and develop them whenever possible and do everything you can not to lose them.

Take a close look at the diagram below, which illustrates the various combinations of values and performance. I have obviously simplified the permutations, as they are infinite, for the benefit of clarity and simplicity.

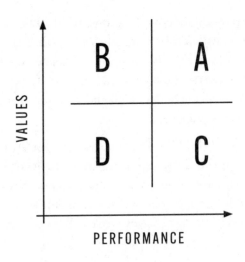

The people who have both low values and low performance – the D-players – are obviously no good to anyone and should be fired immediately. In an ideal world, you should never hire such a person in the first place. With a bit of interview experience, you can learn to spot a D-player early on and prevent this occurrence. But sometimes one slips through the net. As soon as you realise the person can't perform or indeed has the wrong values, you must act swiftly and decisively – no performance-improvement plan will fix this individual. You will simply waste company resources and have a poisonous element infecting other staff. Fire immediately. As my good friend Christian Lommer used to say: "you can't fix stupid".

The people who have high values but low performance – the B-players – are the people in the office who are always friendly and happy, and will make you cups of tea, but they just don't quite get the job done. These individuals have the right values but just can't seem to cut it. It is not that they are not working hard or trying their best. What you really want to do is turn these employees into A-players.

There are really only two things you can do. Either move them to a different role – they may improve if you change their job to one that is better suited to their talents and abilities – or retrain them.

Sometimes the reason for sub-optimal performance can be that they just got a bit stale and bored. Retraining can get them back on track, get them fired up about their career and goals again. Whichever solution or combination you choose, you must leave the employee in no doubt that this is their chance to step up and start delivering the performance you expect as an A-player. There is simply no room for B-players in this company.

In the very early days of starting XLN, I had an employee called Mike Webb in the customer-service department. He was a nice guy, but clearly in the wrong job. When I walked past his desk one morning, I saw that a light on his phone was flashing red and asked him why that was the case. He got very flustered as he realised that he had left a customer on hold for 20 minutes and completely forgotten about it.

Mike and I had a chat where he explained that his real passion was technology and music and that he had only applied for the customer-service role because he desperately needed a job and it was the only opening available at the time. I gave him a job in the technology department where he now looks after all our data and is a very valuable member of the team. He has been with the company for over 17 years now.

Beware the C-player

Now, you need to pay attention because this is the most important thing to know in people management and one of the hardest lessons to learn.

People who do not have values but deliver high performance are the most dangerous. They can literally ruin your company from within and in a very short period of time. They are very tricky to deal with because, when you are their boss, they are difficult to differentiate from an A-player – they look the same when you look at them from your elevated vantage point. The way you deal with them will determine whether you create a mediocre business or a great business.

C-players will deliver a good or often great performance and say all the right things. They will almost always hit their targets and will look like the perfect A-player. But they don't have the values and don't subscribe to your company's way of doing things. They will undermine you behind your back but kiss your behind in public. I call them sunflowers – they have a very large head which moves towards the sun, i.e., you, the boss, and so if you look down at them from above, you will only see their high performance. Their low values will remain hidden.

Only the people below them will see what they are really like. They create shade under and around them and nothing will grow there. Most people have worked for a C-player – someone who takes credit for other people's work, isn't honest or reliable, and plays political games at work. They are very easy to spot when you work for one, but if you employ one, it is much harder, because they deliver the results. And you won't have experienced their bad side because sunflowers always behave impeccably when in your presence.

Very often their performance isn't real anyway. They fudge the sales numbers and set themselves easy targets that they can hit with minimum effort. They are very skilled at deceiving management. If an A-player – and remember these are the good guys you want to build your company around – ends up working for a C-player, you can be sure that they will quickly see through the individual. Often the C-player will try to eliminate the competition by discrediting the A-player. In short order, the A-player will decide they can't work for that individual and, by extension, your company. They will have lost faith in your leadership abilities because they won't be able to reconcile why you would allow the C-player to work in your company. So, the A-player will leave and over time, only other C- or D-players will want to work in that department. It will be rotten to the core and nothing they produce will be real.

No second chances

The important thing to remember about C-players, however, is that one day you will catch them out. You will catch them fiddling the budget or altering targets in their favour. You will find out that some of their sales or results weren't real. You will catch them being dishonest or outright lying, or you will realise that they took credit for someone else's work. They will say they are sorry and that it will never happen again, but really this just means that next time they do something underhand, they will be smarter about it and you won't catch them. Usually, you only get one chance at spotting a C-player. Remember, a leopard never changes its spots.

The problem is that most people will not fire a C-player because they are likely to be the firm's top producer. So they compromise and let them stay. But if you do that, you will have completely undermined the business and everything it stands for, because C-players don't have the right values and are never going to change. The good people working for you will lose all respect for you and your company too.

The minute you spot a C-player you must take action and fire the person. You cannot change someone's values. If their parents couldn't or didn't give them good values by the time they were 16 years old, what chance do you have of changing them now that the person is in their mid 20s or 30s. Don't kid yourself.

Realise that this is the most important management skill to develop. I spend a lot of time sniffing out people that don't fit with our culture. I walk the floor of the business multiple times a day to sense if any individual or department lacks energy or focus. I try hard to spot people that are bad or disruptive elements in the company.

Surround yourself with strong and positive people

I just want to elaborate on this subject a bit more because it is so fundamentally important. Surrounding yourself with the right people can have many consequences in almost every aspect of your life. It is one of the critical keys to lifelong success – whatever that may mean to you now or in the future. I have touched on many of these areas already but will highlight a few of them again.

Subconscious affirmations. We have discussed how critical it is to have the right mindset and the role the subconscious mind plays in that. It therefore equates that if you surround yourself with negative people that constantly focus on their problems, highlight your shortcomings, and generally moan about the world, this will negatively influence your own state of mind. Negativity is a subtle, progressively eroding disease that is guaranteed to affect you to the point where your mindset will affect the world around you. Do not hang around negative people with bad habits. On the contrary, make it a conscious habit to choose the people around you on the basis of a positive and constructive mindset.

Honest feedback is so important, even though it can be painful at times. You do not want to be surrounded by an echo chamber of identical views and opinions. You need people to give you honest, even brutal, feedback and you don't want to discourage that through your reactions. If you end up with people that are too afraid to tell you the truth or indeed hold the exact same viewpoint as you, then you'll likely miss out on the finer nuances and be in danger of sleepwalking into disaster.

Naturally, this has huge implications for how you compose the leadership team that reports directly to you in your business. As I've mentioned before, I try hard to surround myself with colleagues that are complementary in skill set, positive and constructive in mindset, and not afraid to disagree with me.

Now, you can't choose your family, but you can choose your life partner and the friends you have. When I turned 30 years old and decided on a life in recovery, I also had to evaluate my circle of friends. This was mainly due to the habits we shared and the dysfunctional life I was leading. In the end, most of my friends today are not the ones I had back then and that includes my first wife. These decisions are brutal and heart-wrenching but absolutely critical to living a successful and fulfilling life both in business and outside of work.

Chairman and the Board

In business, part of the support structure you have as the CEO, senior management team, and particularly as a shareholder, is the chairman and the Board. In basic terms, the role of the chairman is to hire and fire the CEO and manage the Board. The Board is there to look after the shareholders' interests but also to challenge and support the management team.

I have always looked for a chairman that could fulfil two objectives for me personally (alongside running the Board): to mentor me and share with me their experiences so that I could become a better CEO and businessman. In order for that to work, you have to be completely honest with your chairman, warts and all, otherwise they will be working from incomplete information and, as the saying goes: crap in, crap out.

In business, experience matters because most problematic situations involve people and thus require similar solutions. The same goes for growing a business and how to do that, whether through organic or M&A initiatives; likewise with processes and management. So, I always look for someone who is a mile further down the same path that I am on.

The Board is slightly different. One or more seats are often filled by a private-equity investor, lender or bank. If you have the luxury of being able to choose all the seats yourself, you should take full advantage of that. Do not squander that opportunity by making life as easy for yourself as possible by appointing yes-friends to your board. The board should consist of a diverse group of individuals who all bring something different to the mix. There should be a few people from the leadership team working in the business, someone with banking experience, someone with industry experience, and others with expertise you lack in general.

Whenever our investor has changed, so too has the board and chairman. I have always insisted on choosing the chairman but I do so from a selection put forward by the investor. Initially, say for the first 12–24 months of an investment period, we would have monthly board meetings – ideally in person. Once the investor was comfortable, we would move to meetings every two months, but this is often decided by the investor and based on how well your company is performing.

I believe it is important for the board to focus on the strategic direction of the company while having an eye on day-to-day performance. Looking forward while keeping track of the past, so to speak. I do not like when boards become too operationally involved. I once had the misfortune of working with an investor whose board director would constantly interrupt with random ideas he'd had on the Gatwick Express on his way to the office. If you are running the business well, it is very unlikely that a board member will happen upon something that you haven't already considered. Contemplating such ideas is time consuming and unproductive.

Finally, I've always thought of board meetings as their way of re-evaluating my job as CEO. I prepare comprehensively for board meetings. In particular, I highlight areas that I'm concerned about or where we have a problem so that the board can be a part of the problem or solution. In my experience, it is unwise to spring big problems on an unsuspecting board or to ambush them. Make sure you inform members beforehand if there are thorny issues you want to bring up.

Core Principle 7
Be Yourself

WHEN I WAS in San Francisco learning how to sell, I heard about an old basketball coach who wisely said that you can't be a champ on the court and a chump off the court. What he meant was, you can't be a great guy at work and then go home and be horrible to your family. You can't exhibit two different personas, because it just doesn't work like that. You have to be authentic and true to yourself in any situation because your audience will buy into you as much as they buy into your business or your product or service.

So don't turn up as a different person to different situations, be consistent with who you are and how you react and present yourself. Then people know where they stand with you. And if they like the person they see, they will trust and respect you. What that coach said made a lot of sense to me. This is how I put it into practice.

Be honest

If my wife asks me, does my bum look big in this? I will say, 'yes babe, it does'. If you ask me a question, I will tell you the truth. I will get straight to the point and I will tell you what I think. If I don't want to buy something that you are trying to sell me, I will tell you – and if you ask why, I will tell you that too.

Some people don't like that kind of blunt response, but as I have always told my wife, be careful what you ask me because I will never lie to you. I will always tell you what I think, straight up. Naturally, there's a way of being honest and sometimes a bit of tact or sensitivity is called for. Brutal honesty can still be delivered in a sensitive and appropriate way, and the objective is not to hurt someone's feelings but to foster change and improvement.

Be consistent

A lot of people put on one mask when they go to work and another when they are at home. But I would find that very difficult. It would feel like being two different people. For me, it is too complicated to live a double life; it feels inauthentic. So I have tried to develop a set of morals and work habits that I implement throughout my life. This means that I am the same guy at home as I am at work or on the golf course.

With me, what you see is what you get. There are no surprises and people find that reassuring. Of course, some people don't like me, but that's their business and not mine.

Find out what makes you tick

If you want to be successful, you've got to choose a career that you love or, at a minimum, like doing because if you like doing something, you will spend more time doing it and so will get good at it. And when you get good at something, you like it even more. And so on. It's a virtuous cycle. If you chose something that you inherently dislike doing, then it won't work.

I realised from a young age that what I liked doing best is selling. I am naturally a salesman at heart – I love making money through selling things. I love buying an apple for 50p and selling it for £1. It could be anything too, I don't care what the product is. I have sold Easter-egg decorations, porn magazines, sweets, apples, wine, shirts, perfume, office supplies, telecoms, broadband, Wi-Fi, and energy to name but a few. It will probably be water and insurance next, and then who knows what it might be.

But I also like building things. I realised early on that if you are a great salesperson, you can make a good living, but the amount you sell is determined by how many hours there are in the day. I am not interested in that. I am interested in making money and so, instead of being a salesman myself, I build sales businesses. I build businesses made of people, and because I am doing what I love – and I've worked like a maniac for 30 years – I am now finally pretty good at it. Ultimately, I have become more successful than I ever could have imagined. But remember, enjoying the journey is more important than the destination because the initial destination will inevitably change once you've reached that goal.

Be comfortable with who you are

When you are trying to grow a business and manage a team, you will sometimes have to deal with people who don't see things in the same way as you do, or who even actively disagree with what you are trying to do. They might be colleagues, investors, employees or even customers. It is important to listen to what they have to say, but it is also really important that you are comfortable with who you are and how you deal with things, so that you can be purposeful in the decisions that you make and the direction that you take.

Find a life partner who will let you be yourself

This one is really important. You absolutely have to find someone who is happy to let you be yourself, who is not going to resent all the hours you spend at work, and who is going to understand that when you are not working, you need to switch off and recharge your batteries. If you pick someone whose parents had normal nine-to-five jobs, who were at home at the weekends, who had picnics and did all sorts of family stuff, then you are likely going to run into trouble – that person simply won't understand the way you live your life. There will be a constant battle around you not being home and constantly working.

However, if you marry somebody whose parents were entrepreneurs, were completely absorbed in some creative endeavour or perhaps ran their own business, then you will be fine. This is a life that your partner will know and understand, so they will intuitively and instinctively accept it.

People in Denmark focus a lot on the idea of work-life balance, which means that when I ring my friends there to invite them on a golf trip, they always say that they can't go because they can't get permission from their wives. Whereas my wife, Naima, always says, whatever you need to do to clear your head, that's ok. She has never ever told me that I can't play golf – instead she tells me to go and play because she knows that I will be a much nicer person when I get back.

I play golf every Saturday morning between 8am and 11.30am with a bunch of great friends, many of whom are successful entrepreneurs, and we are all agreed that this is the highlight of our week. It's where we get rid of all the stress and pressure from the week. We always have a great laugh and clear our heads, and if we didn't have that outlet, we would surely go mad.

In fact, not long ago my wife realised that I was getting burned out and so told me to go away on holiday on my own for two weeks to clear my head. So, I went to Vietnam and read books, exercised, ate well, lay by the beach, went for walks, and came back stronger.

The bottom line is that if you want to be successful in business, you simply cannot underestimate the importance of the partner you choose. If I didn't have Naima to look after the house and the kids, to greet me every time I come home with a smile and a kiss, as well as support me, I literally couldn't do what I do.

Stop comparing yourself to other people

I have a fair number of famous friends – actors and golfers, jewellers and film makers, entrepreneurs, bankers and so on – not because they are famous, but because they are great people. And my wife, Naima, has even more famous friends because she was a singer in a very successful R&B band called Honeyz.

But I don't care whether someone is worth £5 or £5bn. One thing I have learnt is that if I measure myself against other people – financially, success-wise, career-wise, house-wise, by how tall I am, how fat I am, or anything really – then half the time I am going to feel inferior, and half the time I am going to feel superior, which is not a nice feeling either. Be happy with who you are and be true to that.

PART
THREE

Putting It
Into Practice

Building A Business

IN THE FIRST two parts, I have hopefully detailed how I managed to create such successful businesses from scratch as well as offered insight into the core principles that underpin everything I do. This is still ground zero though. Now we need to build. In part three, I will be bringing these two aspects together to show how you can start a successful business of your own or grow your existing business into something far greater.

Creating a successful business is not a magical mysterious process, it is actually very straightforward. It's just that there are a dozen obstacles you can run into along the way if you are not careful. I hope I can help you avoid some of the pitfalls that stand in the way of so many entrepreneurs.

Like I said at the beginning of this book, this is my raw and unvarnished advice. It's a compilation of guidance based on my own painful learnings and the things I have been told by my exceptional mentors, friends and business leaders during a career spanning 30 years and counting. It's my tried and trusted model for building companies, leading people and growing businesses. It is my hope that some of the learnings in the following pages will help improve your business and get you firing on all cylinders.

I always say it's hard but not necessarily difficult to build a successful company – well, here's the hard work. Let's get started.

Step 1
Nail Down Your Idea

IT IS FAIRLY easy to come up with a dozen ideas about what kind of business you want to set up, or what kind of products or services you want to sell, but it is a lot harder to come up with an idea that is actually going to make you money. So, you need to be ruthless about which ideas you pursue and which ones you leave to one side. The following is how I do it.

Let an idea ferment

Before rushing headlong into an idea, give it time and space to see if it really has legs. Once I have an idea, I play with it in my head for a few weeks. If the idea passes the longevity test and I am still interested in it, I then write down some back-of-the-envelope numbers – how would we do this? How would that bit work? How much would it cost? What is the structure around this? What would it look like? I think about all these areas and start to see if the idea makes sense on paper. Sadly, ideas don't come fully formed or wrapped up ready to serve, they come in different ways and at different angles. You have to see if they have got what it takes to make it past the first hurdle.

Work out the numbers

Now you need to start looking at whether your idea is actually feasible in financial terms. Look at the numbers that will be involved – the cost of creating or providing the product or service; the number of people you will need to employ to get it off the ground; the cost of marketing it; what kind of profit margins you could expect to get; how many units you could expect to sell; and so on. Does it still look feasible?

The enthusiasm test

So far, so good. My next step is to discuss the idea with a selection of trusted friends, advisors and potential customers. The input I get is really important and goes into the mixing bowl. If, at the end of this process, I am still enthusiastic about the idea, or hopefully even more fired up, then I might be on to something. But if I find my enthusiasm is dwindling the more I talk about it, then I drop the idea.

The reason is that you need to be totally in love with your project – you need to believe in it beyond a shadow of a doubt. Imagine the hundreds of times you will have to explain your idea to suppliers, investors, customers and potential employees. If you haven't got the enthusiasm for it, then they will sense it and you will likely run out of steam. In other words, if your enthusiasm is on a downward trajectory after two months, imagine how you'll feel after 18 months.

Do real market research

If all of these numbers stack up and the idea still looks as though it might be possible, now you need to go out into the market to find out what potential customers think of it. You should be able to work out from their responses whether you will be able to sell sufficient quantities of your product or service to make your business venture worthwhile.

At this point, most budding entrepreneurs will typically ask potential customers something like, 'if I had this product, and it was much cheaper than the one you are using now, or better, would you be interested in buying it? Would you sign up to that service?' And most potential customers will say, 'yes, of course I would'.

But there is a huge difference between that kind of hypothetical research and the real stuff. If I asked a group of people whether they would be interested in switching to a product or service that was 30% cheaper than the one they were currently buying elsewhere, it may be that around 90% of them would say yes. However, if I said to this same group of people, right, sign here on this form and switch to my cheaper product or service right now, only 20% of them would probably do it. That's because suddenly all their fears appear – what if something goes wrong? I don't know you, better the devil you know – and they decide, for whatever reason, that it would be safer to stay with the more expensive provider that they are currently with.

When I was doing the research for XLN, I printed out some forms that looked like a real contract for potential customers to sign. They would actually have to make the commitment there and then to make the switch by signing the form. They weren't legally binding forms, of course, as the company didn't exist. When someone thinks they are signing a form for real and are genuinely committing to making a financial switch, it has a very big influence on their behaviour and their true response is revealed. I managed to sign up four customers to our fictitious telecom service within 2–3 hours. On the back of that real research, I was convinced that I could train an army of salespeople to sign two contracts each during an entire day.

Misleading research is why when most people write business plans they are far too optimistic, both in terms of the amount of sales they hope to get and the amount of time and cost they think it will require. It's far too easy for potential customers to say yes to a new product when there is no risk attached and they know they aren't really going to be asked to buy it. So when I see a business plan, I immediately halve the number of sales it forecasts and double the costs and amount of time it is expected to take. If it still stacks up as a potential business, then it could be interesting.

Did you notice how I took my sales experience of four contracts signed in 2–3 hours and applied it at scale but at a ratio of two sales per eight hours? And even then, that turned out to be slightly on the high side once we had scaled the sales organisation to 50+ agents. Today, the actual number is more like 1.5 sales per day, and it is one of our key KPIs.

You crazy motherf***** - that won't work

A word of warning: when you start talking to friends and family or potential customers, employees and investors, you are going to hear the words 'that won't work' a million times. It is disheartening and brutally disillusioning at times. All I can tell you is that every person who's built a successful business has experienced the same journey. We have all been told that we are wasting our time, that our idea is stupid, and it won't ever work – I have even been told that I am outright insane. Do not let that stop you. Take onboard any constructive points in the criticism, but then move on undeterred.

Often the people that are outright negative about your venture are the types that would never in a million years dare to do something as adventurous as starting a business – or even anything out of the ordinary. Do not let weak or negative people talk you out of pursuing your dream. On the contrary, you should take comfort in the fact that if you are going against the grain, you might just be on to something.

Always seek advice and guidance from people who have built some of the things you are contemplating building. You will hopefully find that most successful entrepreneurs and businesspeople will provide constructive criticism and objective advice, including solutions and potential pitfalls to be aware of.

Don't worry about copycats

When you finally come up with a great idea that looks like it could work, you may find yourself suddenly gripped by another fear – that someone might copy your idea. In reality, or at least in my experience, copying someone's business or idea is a lot harder than it looks. After all, achieving success is not just about the idea, it is down to the execution too.

Many people have tried to copy what we do at XLN. In particular, they have tried to copy our products and pricing, as well as the way we sell. Some competitors have even tried to hire some of our salespeople and replicate our sales models. But I have always been relatively open with people about my ideas, because I know that a great idea on its own is not enough – you can easily screw up a great idea. As I have mentioned before, I will always back a solid management team with an average idea over an average management team with a brilliant idea because an average management team will mess the brilliant idea up and the brilliant management team will change the idea when necessary to find a better way of achieving their goal.

Ultimately, the road to success is long, steep and full of holes. You've got to navigate your way, constantly changing direction, and be prepared to pivot. You have certainly got to get back on your feet many times, so unless you are really good at executing an idea, as opposed to just having it, then you are not going to succeed.

Step 2
Understand Your Audience

I F YOU REALLY want to be successful in business, then you need to know your market inside out. Who are your potential customers? Where are they located? Why should they choose you rather than one of your competitors? If you don't know who your customers are, you will never understand how to sell to them and, more importantly, you will never understand how to keep on selling to them. This is how to do it.

Know who you are selling to

Right from the start, all of XLN's products have been aimed at and specifically designed for small-business customers. That's because, having run many small businesses myself, I knew how important it was for them to be able to keep their costs under control. Even small differences in price could have a big impact on their ability to run their business effectively. Phone calls and broadband, for example, are the absolute lifeblood of any small business today – without them being provided in a cheap and reliable way, a small business simply would not be able to survive.

Knowing the challenges small businesses face every day, I wanted to offer a better price for phone calls than our competitors as well as other products and services they were going to need.

You too need to think very carefully about who is going to buy your product or service, and why. What can you offer them that is better, or faster, or cheaper than what they could get from your competitors? Why would they choose to buy from you? If you don't have a good answer to these questions, then you need to pause and do some hard thinking before you proceed.

Have a product that meets their needs

The underlying aim of any business is to build long-term relationships with its customers – you want your customers to buy from you not just once, but over and over again for many years.

In order to persuade them to do that, you need to have a product or service that they need. A good salesperson can sell anything to anybody once, but you can't build the strong foundations of a business on that. You need to have a product that not only meets their needs now, but will adapt and respond to their changing circumstances in the future, for instance, if their business grows or contracts.

Products or services really fall into two categories:

1. New inventions, or

2. Improvement on an already existing product or service.

I've always focused on the second type of business – probably because I don't have the invention gene. But I do have the improvement gene, so I always look for things to upgrade or otherwise do better.

Whatever you decide to do, it must improve your customer's life for them to be willing to buy it. Maybe it's cheaper, better or generally easier to manage; or maybe you offer a much-improved customer experience. Hopefully it is a number of those things.

I have seen many business plans that incorporate some kind of technology for the sake of it – it was built in a new language or it's a pretty cool piece of tech. The guys with the plan are usually head over heels in love with their invention too. But if the product or service doesn't solve an existing problem, or improve on the current solution, then it won't sell. Stay well away.

Understand what prompts a customer to say yes

Everyone knows that if they switched their electricity supplier then they could save a bit of money, maybe as much as £100–200 a year. But how many times do people wake up in the morning and say, 'right, today is the day I switch my electricity supplier?' They never do. It is just not anywhere on their agenda. Nobody cares about switching their supplier anymore, whether it is for their electricity, gas, mobile phone or whatever. People don't really know how much they spend on these things anyway and it just feels like too much hassle to switch to another provider. It is only when something goes wrong and the supplier screws up, or if the customer can't get through to them on the phone, that they decide they want to change.

So, if you are running a business that is offering a commodity product such as telecoms or energy at a cheaper price than competitors, you need to get people to make the switch by offering them a deal that catches their attention; that encourages them to impulse buy. You obviously have to have a good product at a competitive price, and your salespeople need to be enthusiastic and upbeat, but that is not enough. You have also got to have something you can say that is simple to understand and captures people's attention.

That's why I spend a lot of time thinking about what kind of tariffs and price points are likely to make people notice us. The words 'free' and 'unlimited' are very powerful and if we can give our customers something that they literally can't get anywhere else, that might just motivate them to get in touch.

It's like walking down a supermarket aisle and seeing a fantastic deal on shampoo. You didn't go into the supermarket planning to buy shampoo – it isn't even your usual brand that's on sale – but the deal is so good it catches your eye and before you know it, you have put four litres of shampoo in your trolley. If you can't get a message across that generates a response, you are not going to sell a lot of products.

Make your customers' lives easier

If you can improve the quality of your customers' lives in some way, they will love you forever and never want to leave you.

In the past, customers would pay a fixed amount for line rental and then pay for every single call they made. But I knew from speaking to customers that there was nothing they disliked more than the uncertainty of getting their phone bill each month. They hated the fluctuations in the size of the bill and never knowing how much it was going to be. So I came up with our Free2Call tariff, which looked at the customer's actual usage over the last six months and created a personalised tariff at a fixed price that reflected the average amount of calls the customer made each month.

If the customer's monthly bill would vary between £38 and £48 a month, for example, we would give them a personalised tariff of, say, £42 a month. They would then pay this fixed amount every month, regardless of how many phone calls they actually made, making it easier for them to budget and removing the possibility of receiving a huge bill one month. They wouldn't have to worry about how many calls they made; in fact, they could even start making more calls than usual, for example, if they wanted to start drumming up more business, because it wouldn't cost them a penny more.

The idea has worked so well that now around 90% of our customers are on personalised Free2Call tariffs. It is a great deal both for the customer, which is also easy to understand, and XLN, because we went from having a variable income to having the certainty of a fixed income simply by locking in customers' spending. I love win-win outcomes and think that should always be the aim of every business transaction.

STEP 2: UNDERSTAND YOUR AUDIENCE

Think about how you might be able to make your customers' lives easier. They will be a lot more likely to want to stay with you.

Take them on a journey

A product is not just the thing you are selling, it is the whole package of what your customer experiences when they interact with you. In our case, XLN sell telecoms, payment processing and energy, but our product is the customer's entire journey from their first interaction with us until their last.

It is all about the three Ps: product, people, and processes.

These three elements together are what creates a great business and a great customer experience. It is no good buying a shiny new car if the salesman has added in a lot of options that you didn't need and now you have to overpay for it. You are not going to end up liking that car very much and you certainly won't buy from him again.

The whole journey has to be the best it can be, from the product itself to the sales interaction, the customer service to the technical support. That is the process. If something goes wrong at any point along this journey, then we need to look at why. It could be that one of our people has made an honest mistake – perhaps they accidently pressed the wrong button, or they weren't trained well enough. Or it could be that they have an attitude problem, that they can't be bothered. Or it could be an outdated process that is no longer fit for purpose.

Either way, we need to find out what the problem is and deal with it promptly. That is why I give all our customers my personal email address, because I take the view that if one person has taken the time to write to me about an issue, then there will be many others who are in the same situation and, for whatever reason, haven't written to me. It is a red flag telling us that something isn't right, and it needs to be dealt with promptly and efficiently.

Be responsive to your customers' changing needs

Over time, the way that we use the phone has changed. In particular, the relationship between how we use a fixed landline and how we use mobile phones has changed. For our customers who bought a package from us offering unlimited calls using their landline, it meant that they were actually paying twice for some of those business calls. This is because customers would sometimes use their mobile instead of their landline office phone, and thus incur charges from their mobile-phone operator, for a call they could have made for free on their XLN tariff. That didn't seem fair. So we developed a SIM-only mobile offering that was part of their Free2Call tariff. In other words, our unlimited-call plan could now be used on both devices at no extra cost. We even threw in unlimited text messages for free.

XLN customers could now make 'free' calls on their mobile phone because it was part of their office package. They then had the option of adding a data package at the same time to enable them to open their emails and access data content and the internet on their mobile phone. Again, at prices similar to what you'd pay for a Tesco mobile package but with our great customer service included.

It was a nice gesture on our part, but it was also an immensely pragmatic one too. If we had stuck rigidly to only offering landline calls, we would have lost our customer's mobile business to a competitor, who might then have sought to take their landline calls away from us too. But by including mobile calls in our deal, we not only take over our customers' mobile-phone requirements, we also sever their relationship with a rival telecoms operator. Genius.

Stay one move ahead

Some time ago, I realised that Wi-Fi networks would have an increasingly important role to play in the future. After all, people were using their smartphones more and more, and the content they accessed became more and more data hungry. Five years ago, you wouldn't have dreamed of looking at a video on your phone because it would be buffering all the time and be super expensive. Now, people do it all the time.

The problem is that if everyone started looking at a high-definition (HD) video on their phone at the same time, the mobile networks would start creaking. I realised that the rapid rate at which our collective consumption of data was growing meant that it would not be possible for mobile technology to keep up. Even when 5G is launched and initially delivers overcapacity, that will soon get soaked up by higher bandwidth definition and more data-hungry applications.

I felt that the best way to handle these data requirements would be to offload them through Wi-Fi onto the fixed fibre-optic network, because it would always be practically unlimited. So we started opening Wi-Fi hotspots across the country. We now have the biggest free public Wi-Fi network in the UK, with 20,000+ hotspots up and down every high street.

This not only gives us the potential to do some interesting capacity deals with other mobile-phone operators in the future, it also enables us to deliver a fantastic service to our small-business customers right now.

It means we are the first telecoms business to offer free public Wi-Fi to 20,000 of our small-business customers who own high-street businesses and would really benefit from it. A range of restaurants, hairdressers, cafés, and sandwich shops can all now offer free public Wi-Fi on their premises so that, for example, someone in the hairdressers can watch a film on Netflix on their smartphone while they are having their hair done.

It is well established that customers tend to go to places which offer free Wi-Fi, so this is helping our small-business customers run their businesses better by offering their customers a free service. We will eventually have to charge more for the service – as it is currently costing us £1m a year to provide – but the charge will still be a fraction of the cost of them providing Wi-Fi to their customers themselves.

The benefit to our customers is an additional service that makes their life easier and helps their business for a few extra pounds a month; the benefit to us is that the more services we can provide to our customers, the more XLN becomes an integral part of their business life. My ambition is for XLN to become a trusted partner for small businesses, a place where they can get all of their non-essential business services like telecoms, card processing, energy, insurance, CCTV, and productivity apps.

Consider how your business might be able to stay one move ahead of the competition.

Don't keep customers tied to you against their will

We don't have rolling contracts at XLN because I am not interested in trying to hold onto customers who don't want to stay with us. I want them to stay with us because we offer them the best deal. As long as our products are great, our pricing is amongst the cheapest in the market, and our customer service is world class, then I don't see why a customer would want to leave us.

If I can't convince someone to stay with us by giving them great value, unbelievable customer service and great products, what reason do I even have to be in the market? As it happens, some customers end up leaving us because they have been promised nirvana by an overzealous competitor, but it is my belief that in the long term they will return to us once they realise they were sold a pup and XLN is the best place for them.

Don't spend your time focusing on ways to stop your customers leaving – focus instead on finding ways to make them want to stay.

Make them want to talk to you

Don't sell steak, sell sizzle. When you walk into a restaurant and smell the barbeque and the garlic and hear the sizzle, that is what makes your mouth water – not when they come and show you a big cold piece of meat.

In the same way, when you are sending an email to a prospective customer about a new product or service you are launching, don't tell them every last detail about it, just give them the highlights of how it will improve their life. They will then want to call you to find out more. Every campaign we run, whether by email, Facebook or some other social media channel, has one purpose: to get people to talk to us.

That's because we want to have the opportunity to talk to potential customers about how our product or service works and explain what it can do for them and what it includes. They can then be sure that they are signing up to the most appropriate, cost-effective package for them.

Make your customers' happiness your number one priority

My aim is simple: I want to give our customers the best overall deal that they can get anywhere in the country.

This is primarily because I have almost 500 employees who are all dependent on me – if we look after our customers, they will look after our employees. My employees will then look after the business and the shareholders. If you look after your customers and employees, the rest will take care of itself.

Step 3
Build Great Sales Teams

STRONG SALES TEAMS have always been the building blocks of my various businesses. They underpin every aspect of our success and provide a robust framework to drive the company forward. But most businesses can't see that.

Businesses that make money by selling – whether online, on the phone or in person – typically focus on developing brilliant individual salespeople. But there are two problems with taking this approach. First, you can't really build a large team of brilliant salespeople because there simply aren't enough of them. They would be a nightmare to manage anyway because great salespeople can often act like prima donnas. Second, and perhaps more importantly, brilliant salespeople pretty much always end up in the same place. As their skills and ability develop, the effort they put in decreases because they now know how to do the job. They become lazy. Their income remains pretty much the same and eventually their bad habits catch up with them – these great salespeople crumble and disappear.

So, at XLN, instead of creating great individual salespeople, we have chosen to create great sales teams instead. We focus on developing new leaders and managers, not salespeople. This is a very different approach. We believe that if we do this, the sales will take care of themselves.

A great sales team is not made up of a bunch of great salespeople, but of good salespeople who can do a consistent number of sales every month and make it look fun and easy. If they can do that, they can help us train new people, which will grow the team, the department and the business. That is why I always focus on the idea of promotion and progression rather than production. If you talk about production, you get sales people, but I want sales leaders to grow the business, and hence I always talk about progression and promotion.

This is how to create a great sales team.

Make sure your team really knows their stuff

A salesperson needs to know their pitch and their product knowledge inside out, they need to know how to handle concerns about the price or the product that might be raised by potential customers, and they need to know the processes and systems that the business uses. I am absolutely fanatical about this, because learning these things is not a question of intelligence, it is simply a question of having the right attitude and putting some hours in. Your team needs to study them every morning and every evening until they know them off by heart – and if they don't, you need to let them go.

Stop the rot early

When someone starts working for you, you have to assume that in their first three weeks you will be getting their absolute best behaviour – they will want to show you that they are a good employee. So, if they are lazy, have a bad attitude or no enthusiasm in these first three weeks, then it is pretty obvious what they are going to be like in three months or three years. Don't kid yourself that they are suddenly going to be hit by lightning and have a revelation in month 16. Cut your losses and let them go.

Focus on driving productivity

If most of the people in your sales team aren't making a good living then you have got a problem, because they will leave. You will then be endlessly churning people and your team won't be able to grow, or even find some sense of shared culture and stability. So, it is really important that your employees are making money, and they are only going to make money if they have good productivity.

You have to take the person who used to do 25 sales a month, for example, and figure out how you get them to do 30 sales a month. Then you need to embed these new habits and motivate them to do 30 sales every month, come rain or shine, until they consistently hit that level of sales productivity. You will find that some months they will do 33, 34, or even 40 sales.

Productivity and sales success produces a dynamic and high-performing sales team.

Encourage consistency

Consistency is key to growth, and you need to have consistent performance and production to be able to grow a team. In fact, this is so important that I would rather someone achieved a consistent number of sales every day or week or month than have wildly differing sales numbers, even if they are not doing as many sales overall in the period. That's because you can't build on inconsistent sales performance. Consistent production comes from having consistent work habits, consistent attitude, consistent enthusiasm and consistent effort. If all of these are consistent, then the results will be consistent, and you will have something to work with. Until someone is consistent, you cannot help them improve.

Decent salespeople with good work habits can actually outperform really good salespeople over time, because they are consistent. Someone who can do 35 sales month in, month out, will beat a more talented person who might do 50 sales one month, but then 20 the next. Over time, inconsistent sales performance only goes in one direction: downwards.

Make sure your team always has a great Monday

Your number-one objective is to ensure that your sales teams have a great Monday. If they have a horrible Monday, they will be pushing uphill for the rest of the week. And you really don't want that.

When people are worried about numbers, they become desperate and so will not present the confident front that is needed to sell. So having a brilliant Monday is absolutely critical. If you count your sales on a monthly basis then, likewise, you must have a great start to the month. I don't believe in quarterly sales goals as they are too long term and difficult for the average tenured sales agent to comprehend.

How do you create a great Monday?

First, you call all your team on Sunday afternoon and make sure that they are mentally and physically prepared for Monday morning. Then you get them into the office early so that you can get them fired up and focused before they start making phone calls or seeing potential customers.

However, all that energy and enthusiasm will only last them from 9am to 11am – if they haven't sold by then, they will start to go downhill. So, you also have to do everything you can to ensure that they start bringing in sales in those first two hours, because otherwise you will have to start giving people their confidence and 'juice' back at 11am.

Take control of the mood

If no-one is managing to sell anything, it is time to take people off the phones and start getting them jazzed up. You need to take their eye off the ball because they are likely all thinking that they are going to have a really bad sales day. Nobody can sell anything with that attitude, so you need to get them focusing on something else which will bring back their intensity and enthusiasm.

You could hold a contest, which is something that we often do at XLN. Announce that whoever makes the most sales pitches in the next hour will win £50, for example. Then all of them will get back on the phones to start making calls and suddenly you will have got that intensity back, because now they are not thinking about making sales, instead they are thinking, 'right, I'm going to win that £50 by speaking to more people in the next hour than anybody else'. And I guarantee that bang, sales will start pouring in.

Keep the momentum

If someone on your team makes a sale, get them to keep on making calls. They will be full of confidence and genuine enthusiasm and potential customers will be able to sense that and will respond to that. Most people do the opposite, however, and take a break or go and get a coffee after a successful sale. Then they return to their desk ten minutes later with all of their enthusiasm gone, and have to start winding it up again. This is a big mistake. As soon as someone has made a sale, get them to make another 20 calls while they are at their most powerful.

Beware the old timers

The people that drain you the most are not the new people who are full of enthusiasm and energy, but the 'old dogs' who are late because it was raining outside. Or say they haven't done any sales yet because the market has changed. They are full of excuses; they know how to game the system, they know how to play you, and they will drain you emotionally with all their BS. Think about it – how is it possible for a brand new person to do three sales in a day when you have an experienced salesperson moaning about how hard it is to complete three sales in three days?

The main ingredients that generate sales are hard work, great work habits, enthusiasm, and sales technique. Often salespeople who have been in the same job for a while don't have the enthusiasm they need, nor do they put in the hours or the intensity.

As manager of the team, this is where you need to be really careful, because you can quickly get burnt out dealing with people like this. You will start believing all their excuses and it will make you weak. And then their production will decrease even more, to the point where they are not really making any money, and they will blame you and quit. Eventually, the team will collapse and your business will be in trouble. You would have blown the biggest opportunity in your life just because you listened to old timers.

Don't be afraid to make tough decisions

If somebody steals, lies or mis-sells, it is pretty easy to deal with because their actions are unacceptable – they have to leave. But what do you do with somebody who does 30 sales on a monthly basis, but doesn't work particularly hard?

The answer is, if you can't get them to work harder, then you need to let them go. Having someone with a bad attitude and bad work habits will poison your team and stop it from being able to grow.

I would rather have somebody with a great attitude who is working really hard than somebody with an iffy attitude who is working a little bit and doing 30 or 40 sales. The hardest decision a business leader will ever be faced with is getting rid of high-performing people who aren't displaying the right work habits and values. It can be tempting to focus on the loss of those 30 or 40 sales and believe that your business will fall behind without them. Don't be weak and think like this.

Well, maybe your business might fall behind. But often, when you get rid of these people, your team will experience a natural breath of fresh air and production will subsequently increase. The fact is that, if you keep people with bad attitudes on your team, then you will never be able to grow the team. But if you fire them, then the team can grow and will have a future.

Tough love

We used to say: "nobody leaves because you are too tough on them; they leave because you are too weak". Certainly, when dealing with sales teams, you need to understand that it is better that they hate you from Monday to Friday but love you on payday than the opposite.

It is not a popularity contest – your job is to ensure that your team makes as much commission as possible. That will inevitably mean pushing them hard and accepting no excuses or lack of results. My own experience was that I, through sheer hard work and long hours, was able to quadruple my results from one week to the next. Therefore, my firm belief is: "if I can do it, you can do it".

Thinking that people leave because you are too nice as a manager is perhaps counterintuitive. But look at it this way: the agent doesn't put in enough effort and gets poor results, and you have accepted their performance without doing anything about it. Then payday arrives, the agent turns around and says, "sorry Boss but I'm going to have to leave because I can't pay my bills".

Who's the winner here? You both lost!

Tough love is necessary in all aspects of business and life. You will find that people management is not too different from parenting. You are the disciplinarian, and sometimes tough love is called for. Do not be afraid to use it, but always remember we are not talking about intimidation, or any form of physical or verbal abuse.

Personal interest

I have found that one of the most effective ways to manage people is by taking a personal interest in them. This manifests itself in various ways.

The first thing you can take a personal interest in is to determine what each person on your team is motivated by. In other words, what are their goals? What do they hope to accomplish with your company? What turns them on? What are their hot buttons? Once you are aware of these keys to motivation, you can begin to work towards helping them achieve their goals. Until you know exactly what it is that each person works for, you can do very little to point them in the right direction or get them back on track should they fall off course. It is important to constantly remind the person of their goals and hence why they should be putting forward a huge effort.

Each day, the people in your sales team will experience new things. Some will be positive, others negative. Therefore, it is essential that you make contact with each of your people on a daily basis. If possible, this should be done in person, but if that is not possible then be sure to invest ten minutes in a phone call. You don't want any negative input gained during the day to be lingered over. You want to be on the ball and timely in helping your team members overcome negative influences or trying situations.

On the other hand, if a team member has had a good day, you should be the first to congratulate them and show that you are just as interested in positive influences as you are in dispelling negative ones.

Another effective aspect of this kind of motivation is to get out on the front line with your people. You must be a good example to your team. It is far better to show them what it is you want them to do rather than tell them what it is they should be doing. Remember, this is your business, and you want to develop a strong nucleus that will become the backbone of your company. Also, by working with them in the field, you can assure yourself that they are capable of doing the job properly. Once again, I refer to some of the great habits Frank McKay taught me. While CEO at Travis Perkins, Frank would regularly turn up unannounced to one of their 1,200 branches.

Your involvement in your team will take many forms. Business in the office, business in the field, socialising, etc. However, irrespective of the form of your interaction, you must work hard to maintain a fine line between yourself and your team; you are, after all, an authority figure. It is much better for you to earn their respect by showing them that you are sincerely interested in their career and their success within the company.

Let them know that your success is a direct result of theirs.

The truth about negative motivation

In sales, a great deal of time and effort is spent working your team into a frenzy by dangling carrots, giving away your hard-earned money in bonuses, painting a beautiful picture of a salesperson's potential future, running contests, and doing other uplifting, positive things. All too often, however, your efforts to motivate probably leave you dismayed with the lack of results.

Why is it that the same people keep winning all the bonuses, usually through delivering as many sales as they would when there are no bonuses up for grabs?

Why is it that Steve, who you have been grooming for a management role, suddenly drops out?

Why is it that so many people just bursting with potential never live up to your expectations?

Maybe your problem is the same one that befalls many sales managers in many different kinds of businesses. People, in general, do not always react positively to positive forms of motivation because they are never told that there is a downside that may affect their future. Undoubtedly, you know that there are two basic motivating factors in life: gaining a benefit and avoiding a loss. Why is it, then, that sales managers everywhere are afraid to develop a 'fear of loss' concept with their salespeople?

I think sales managers, of both salaried and commission-only roles, are afraid that if they inject fear of loss into the equation, their salespeople will stop working – just down their tools and quit in droves. In actuality, and in my experience, the opposite is true.

Part of the problem is that sales managers fail to realise just how great the opportunity they provide is. Certainly with our structure, the XLN opportunity is incredible. We give average people, some without any form of experience, the opportunity to be fully trained and work within a company where hard work is rewarded equally, and quick progression is possible based entirely on merit. All anyone really needs is a hunger to succeed.

Whatever product or service you may be selling, and whatever sales structure you've devised, I'm sure that you have put a lot of effort into providing the best product for your team to sell as well as the best career opportunity for them to progress in life. With this knowledge in hand, you must develop enough pride to be disappointed when people do not take advantage of it or put the effort in, regardless of their reasons or, rather, their excuses.

There are thousands of people out there who are looking for an opportunity in sales. There is no reason why you should allow people to carry your sales materials and tie up territory if they are not sincere in their efforts. Therefore, you must inject this philosophy into their brains.

You must expect people who are representing your company to take full advantage of the chance you have given them. If you allow anyone to work in your company while looking for something better to do, you are doing a disservice to yourself and the rest of the people in your organisation. This is what negative motivation is all about. Injecting that fear of loss. In actuality, you are saying: 'look, either take this job seriously or hand in your notice so I can give the role to someone who really wants to make it big in life'.

Negative motivation is not a negative thing. It is just a way of letting everyone know that you expect them to appreciate the opportunity and, if they do not or will not, there is a downside – namely, being relieved of the chance of working in your company.

Tying it all together

The following example should tie together many of things I have mentioned in this chapter.

If you are in sales, whether field based or over the phone, then you need to understand this equation:

Hours worked × intensity × pitch = sales results

So, the more hours you work (everything else being the same), the more sales you will make.

The level of intensity you work with is critical and takes different forms. Obviously, if you only speak to ten prospects per hour, then you would do half the number of sales than if you spoke to 20 prospects per hour. But intensity is more than that. If you aren't enthusiastic, don't have the right tone of voice, body language or energy, you will not connect or enthuse as many of the prospects as you otherwise would. Hence, less sales.

A sales pitch is comprised of multiple parts, things like the introduction, the story, features and benefits, objection handling, hook and close. Everything depends on your pitch, your product and the way you do things, but the principles I'm talking about remain the same. If a salesperson gets stuck at any stage of the pitch funnel, their conversion rate will suffer. Only focused practice and experience can improve this.

The very first thing I do with new salespeople is to tell them that long hours and hard work with intensity are mandatory. I tell them upfront that it is going to be the hardest thing they've ever done.

Then I instil a work ethic that ensures they work at least a full eight hours on the phone or in the field – not including travel to and from work/territory or lunch breaks. It shouldn't take too long to get the agent up to this level of effort. Sometimes another few hours of work might be called for, so I plant those seeds early as well.

My next objective is to build the salesperson up to pitching to 20+ prospects per hour. They may initially only be able to complete six or eight pitches per hour, but you should challenge them to reach a higher number at every opportunity.

The final part of the puzzle is to make sure their pitch is so good that most conversations finish with a closing attempt. If you don't close, you won't sell.

Developing the habit of working a full eight hours while pitching to 20+ prospects an hour takes some time, but can be done. I insist on the individual practising their pitch, product knowledge, systems and processes, and objection handling at home and during weekends. Naturally, while developing the first two habits we can also gain experience and practise pitching.

The time it takes for an average person to start doing one sale per day is around five weeks. If that is their first goal, or what they focus on, then it can easily seem very far away. Tell your salespeople not to focus on the numbers; that sales are the result of their input. Make them look at the equation again and realise that they can control the first part through their actions, but they can't control the outcome.

Why focus on the outcome when it's the input that matters?

The input will directly correlate to the results they get out. In other words, if they work the full eight hours, speaking to 20+ prospects an hour with intensity, and their pitch is great, they will get amazing results. So, let's work on that and celebrate the incremental improvements in those parts of the sales process.

As a manager, this is what you do. Keep a daily score sheet of hours a new salesperson has worked and see that they continue to push towards the full eight hours. Celebrate every daily improvement towards that target.

Likewise, keep a daily score of how many prospects your agent speaks to in an hour. Initially, this might only be six or seven potential customers. But you can work on the various components that allow the agent to increase the number spoken to and, most importantly, you can celebrate any improvements at multiple times during the day. So rather than saying, "today your target is one sale", you should be saying, "today we want to get to seven hours of talk time and we want to speak to at least 11 prospects per hour".

This will refocus our efforts on the input and offer us smaller, incremental goals that can be hit and celebrated. The agent will be motivated by every success and the recognition they receive. You should celebrate publicly so that others in your team or in the department can benefit from the increased enthusiasm and feelings of progression and success. If you celebrate and reward behaviour like this, then it is only human nature for everyone else to also want that kind of recognition.

When it comes to the pitch, there will be multiple levels of conversion that you must optimise. If, for example, the agent doesn't manage to engage many prospects in conversation and most of their calls are very short, it is likely because their introduction is poor. Are they 'smiling' and enthusiastic? Do they have the right intro and tone of voice? Do they take control of the conversation?

You may pitch things differently from what I'm alluding to, and you should obviously do what works for your product and company, but the methodology is the important take away. Once you have refined your agent's introduction and they can engage more prospects in conversation, you move on to the next stage of the pitch funnel.

Eventually, you will have instilled great work habits in the agent and upskilled the agent to a level where the sales start rolling in. And all the while, you will have focused on celebrating their incremental daily improvements. All going well, the subsequent sales success will lead to promotion in your sales organisation.

Only ever focus on the inputs you can control. The rest will take care of itself.

Step 4

Create A Strong Culture

IF YOU WANT to build a successful business, you need to give it a strong identity. That means creating a unique culture that is instantly recognisable and understood not just by the people who already work there, but by everyone who joins the business as it grows.

This culture is led from the top and should reflect the nature of the work and the aspirations of the business. It is reinforced each day by every aspect of what happens there, from how people dress to the way they work.

Culture is not just a nice thing to have, it is an essential component of every successful business. It creates a bond or a motivating force that unites people and gets them working together as a team.

Here's how to create a strong culture in your business.

Culture starts on day one

Potential employees start getting an idea of the culture of your business from the very first moment they have contact with it. When somebody reads a recruitment advert for XLN, for example, they have an immediate sense of the kind of company we are and the kind of culture we have.

It helps that our recruitment adverts have always been a bit different. In the early days, for example, we would run tiny adverts the size of a postage stamp in newspapers such as the *Evening Standard* or the *Manchester Evening News*. They wouldn't give the name of the company, they would simply have a catchy headline saying something like 'Life's a Beach', 'Fun and Games' or, 'New Year, New

Career'. The rest of the advert would be fairly blank. We deliberately didn't want to give people a lot of information, because the whole point of the advert was to get potential employees to pick up the phone and call us, so that we could then pitch to them on the phone.

But that was only the start of it. When they called us, we would say as little as possible on the phone too. This would mean that potential staff would actually have to come in and see us. Only once they were at the office in the orientation session, would we reveal how XLN worked. We did it this way because we knew that the very best way of explaining what XLN did and how we did it was for people to come and see it for themselves.

For this to work effectively, there had to be consistency between the ads, the phone interview and the first meeting to ensure that the culture was continually being reinforced. As a result, by the time people started work, they would have a very clear sense of what XLN was all about.

You too need to think about what sort of impression your business is making on people, whether they are potential employees, investors, suppliers or customers, right from the very first moment they encounter it. Are you giving out a consistent message? And does it accurately reflect the way your business operates?

Foster a climate of hard work

Unless people are prepared to work long hours and do whatever it takes, they are not going to succeed at XLN. In fact, they should not even bother applying for the job, because they will be kicked out within a week. I don't need people who are nine-to-fivers, I need people who get things done every single time. If someone wants to succeed, they need to be ready and willing to put in the hard work and long hours – and occasionally work at weekends too.

I was taught to work hard and that is the reason why I have achieved so much. I work two or three times as many hours as most other people and if you do that for 30 years in a row, you get somewhere. It's that simple.

If you truly want your business to succeed, then you not only need to work hard yourself, you also need to ensure that all your teams are working hard too. When Jeff Bezos started Amazon and was interviewing prospective employees himself, he would always tell them: "You can work hard, long or smart but at Amazon.com you can't choose two out of three". I love that.

Our sales strategy is not up for discussion

There is only one way of running the XLN sales programme and I am not asking people who join the business to add their personal touch to it. Put bluntly, I don't want their input or their suggestions.

While this goes against my usual advocation for an open atmosphere, this is different. I had the good fortune to be trained by some of the best sales leaders in the world; I then spent 30 years tweaking the system for the UK and the kind of markets we sell to, as well as the people we recruit. So, without wishing to sound arrogant, we have perfected, almost at least, a way of developing salespeople, managers and leaders that is second-to-none. So, our strategy is not up for discussion.

If someone wants to be successful at XLN, they need to learn our way of doing things. Only once they've mastered that will I be open to their suggested improvements. I am not looking for people who will only complete 65% of the programme because they don't agree with the other 35%. They either learn it 100% our way or we need to agree to disagree and part ways as quickly as possible. It is my way or the highway in this regard.

Of course, every programme can be improved, but clarity of vision and mission is so important that you will achieve more through enforcing a simple message than by allowing confusion to arise and constant change to occur. Stick to your guns and keep reinforcing the programme you have decided upon.

Develop a culture of candour

Beyond strategy discussions, you want a culture where people are not afraid to disagree with you. The last thing you want is a team of 'yes men' around you.

As the boss or leader, you have a certain inherited authority that comes with your position within the company, but you mustn't let that stifle honest debate and rigorous argument. You are not always right, and the best argument should always win the day. If you don't consciously work to encourage debate, it will be very easy for people to just agree with you, which is lethal in the long run. You need honest, sometimes lively, debate to ensure all the arguments have been presented and all angles have been covered, so that you don't sleepwalk into a pothole that could have been avoided.

Having said that, once a direction is embarked on, you shouldn't allow people to divert you from the agreed course because they don't agree with it or don't want to play their part. When I encounter that kind of attitude, I'm very clear that if the employee disagrees and doesn't feel they can support our objectives, then they are free to find another company that better fits their beliefs. See you later.

You get what you reward

Whatever culture you want to foster, remember that what you reward is what you will get more of. In other words, if you recognise someone for disagreeing with you and soberly presenting alternative views, then they will do more of that in the future. Likewise, if you shoot someone down because they dared to contradict you, then everyone else will see that and quietly resolve not to disagree with the boss because the downside is too painful and there is no upside. That's the beginning of rot setting in and your team dissolving.

If you don't believe how powerful this distinction is, next time someone tells a joke, you should say, "that was funny; you always make me smile". I guarantee that going forward that individual will try to crack a joke whenever you are together. Similarly, I always tell some people in the sales department: "you are the spark plug in this department. You are always fired up and enthusiastic". They almost always continue to display this important behaviour which is so critical within a sales environment.

Promote from within

It is far better to develop your own managers and leaders from within the business than to bring new people in from other companies, because your existing employees already live and breathe your culture and the way that you do things. Unless someone has grown up with the system you have created, they will never truly understand how it works. By promoting from within, you will know exactly who you are dealing with and that you have someone who is already steeped in the way your business does things.

The great thing about wanting to continually develop more sales leaders within the business is that this is what our employees want too. Most people in sales would like to move up to management at some point, so you need to offer people a clear and realistic path to doing this. Otherwise, they will burn out and you will lose your best people. When you consistently promote from within, it will become obvious to your salespeople that there are real promotion opportunities for them.

In turn, if you constantly talk about getting people promoted, then you don't have to talk about hitting sales goals. All you have to say is that you need to get them promoted to the next level and they will instinctively understand that such a promotion will require effort and the attainment of whatever is next on their agenda.

Of course, in order to be able to promote from within, you need to be in a position to offer people more senior roles. And that means you need to be continually growing your business. The difference between XLN and a lot of other companies is that we always want to grow. You should too.

Reward people well

We have a very clear philosophy within XLN: XLN is everyone's business. It belongs to everyone that works here. So, the people who create value for the business get to keep part of that value – the more value they create, the more they get to keep for themselves.

More than 40 XLN managers have equity in the business and, as a result, many of them have become millionaires. I'm very proud of that.

Step 5
Be An Effective Leader

L EARNING HOW TO manage people is one of the hardest things you will ever have to learn in business – particularly if many of them started out as friends. But you need to learn how to do it well, otherwise your business will never develop the structure and focus it needs. This is how to do it.

Don't be afraid to expect great things from people

You are only going to get brilliant people working for you if you set them the expectation that they are going to be brilliant. Diamonds are pieces of coal that have withstood great pressure over a long period of time, after all.

We are trying to take young people with little or no experience and turn them into great sales leaders. And while we are very good at it, we also know that you don't make great people in a lax environment, you make them in a hard-core pressure-cooker environment. This is about taking average people and turning them into above-average people; it is about taking ordinary people and making them extraordinary. This, of course, applies to all departments and not just salespeople.

Set your employees high goals that are challenging yet realistic and measurable. And make them specific, so you can accurately gauge success – you need to have something you can visualise, something you can attain.

Lead by example

Never expect an employee to do something that you wouldn't be prepared to do yourself, whether that is fixing a chair or cleaning a toilet. And don't just tell them, show them how it should be done. If you are trying to show someone how to sell a product over the phone, for example, then start by making phone calls yourself and let them listen in. People will be much more prepared to follow your orders when they know that you are not asking of them anything that you couldn't or wouldn't readily do yourself.

You should be the first to arrive in the morning and you should be the last to leave. A boss that swans in from time to time is a cancerous influence and will set the wrong example.

One great benefit that comes from having built a company from the ground up is that you know what's involved in most roles – you've more than likely done every job at some point. And so when it then comes to delegating responsibilities, you inherently know what's involved in each role and what kind of effort and time you should expect a certain project or job to take. Nobody is then able to pull the wool over your eyes and convince you that the job takes eight weeks when, in reality, it could easily be done in three weeks.

What's the job of a great CEO?

Obviously, the role of a CEO covers a great many things, but I see the main jobs falling under three key areas.

1. Create and clearly communicate the vision

Everybody wants to be part of something bigger than themselves; they want to belong to a group of like-minded and enthusiastic people. Hence, it is your job as CEO to communicate your vision clearly so that everyone understands what it is you are all collectively trying to achieve. Having a mission of 'let's all get as rich as possible' is not going to cut it. It must be something more ethereal and meaningful, like, 'we want to provide our small business customers with the best products and customer service in the UK'.

2. Provide visible leadership

Be visible, available and approachable. Walk the floor; make time to talk to people; leave your office door open; encourage, reward and recognise people for their efforts. Focus on the positive contributions and the desired work habits that you notice displayed by individuals.

3. Solve problems

Business is really all about solving problems. As a leader or the CEO, you are essentially synthesising a constant flow of information into either strategy or daily actions that need to be taken to move the business forward.

In the early stages of a company's life, it is really important that you are able to fix problems on the fly. Until a business matures, you will not have all the people and processes in place to ensure the smooth running of things. Problems or major fires will pop up constantly and unexpectedly, and it's up to you to solve these in collaboration with your team.

A calm, rational, positive and constructive demeanour is definitely advantageous, but I totally get that it's sometimes very hard to maintain such an attitude when you've got your entire future riding on a business' success. But starting to emotionally disintegrate in front of your team is counterproductive and should be avoided at all costs. So is blaming people and shouting, as that just adds more fear to an already volatile environment.

During a crisis, and you will encounter many, my best advice is to stay calm and collected, as that is what your team really needs from you. Then, organise everyone's suggestions to arrive at the best course of action.

Understand that managing millennials requires a different approach

We have a few hundred millennials working at XLN. They all arrive with a different sense of reality to older generations and that means they require a different management style.

Perhaps the most obvious reason they see life differently is because they are the first generation to have grown up with mobile phones, the internet and, most crucially, social media. That means that the way they look at gratification and reward is completely different to the way that previous generations looked at it.

When I was a child, I had to wait a week for Columbo to come on the television. Now, whatever you want to watch, you can watch – everything is available more or less instantly.

Our millennial employees literally have their mobile phones lying next to them when they work, and they pretty much have a finger on it all the time. And if my managers ban them from having their phone next to them, they simply put it on their legs so they can feel it vibrate when a message comes in. And, of course, that happens every ten minutes or so. How can you concentrate when you are constantly being distracted? It's not possible.

This continuous access to social media has changed their aspirations and their priorities too. They all want to change the world, like Mark Zuckerberg has done. They want to make the world all green and save the dolphins too. And they want to do it all this week.

That is all very admirable, but millennials, from my experience, tend to lack a sense of perspective and scale about the kind of things they think might be possible. I see these young people start work and become a little bit despondent; they are disinterested and disengaged, and before long, they become frustrated and depressed. And then they say, 'I have already been here for three months and I am not going anywhere'. Or they say, 'I have been here for six months and

I haven't made a big impact on the business'. Or complain that they 'haven't made a mark on the company'. And I'm like, chill. I was the most impatient person when I was younger, but even I knew that you needed to put some work in to achieve results.

The way that millennials see the world of work has meant that I have had to change our approach. Back in the early days of XLN, when people only worked on commission, I had to dangle carrots to encourage people to stay. One of them was quick progression and quick promotion. So, I have taken a leaf out of that approach and adapted it for our new recruits, and we have now rolled it out to a lot of different departments.

When we hire and train people now, we make sure that each part of the process correlates to a promotion in the business. This means that every time something new is achieved, the salesperson is rewarded with a certificate, congratulated, and promoted to the next level. As a result, we have added two or three levels in between our normal promotional levels.

Although this is only a small thing to the company at large, it means that our young people feel like they are moving up through the business, which makes a big difference to them. You could argue that they are not actually moving on any quicker than before, but they feel as though they are and therein lies the genius. For me, it is always about continuous incremental improvement – whether that is in sales, process improvements, or learning new skills and habits. The smaller the bites, the easier they are to swallow and the sooner the gratification.

Accept that as the business grows your relationships will change

When you are starting a business, you will often find yourself becoming friends with the people you work with, simply because there are only a few of you and you spend so much time together. You work long hours and become really close because you hang out and sit in the office drinking beer and eating pizza together. Indeed, you probably spend more time with them that you do with your family. The fact that you are going through some really tough and traumatic experiences at the same time brings you quite close. And when you are starting a business from scratch, this kind of bonding is important. You are not paying people particularly well, so you have to build some sort of social connection to hold onto them.

But as the business grows, you have to change your management style, because now it is not a little intimate group of eight or 12 people, it is 50 people, and you are the boss. You still know everyone's name, but you have got to start putting a bit of structure in place. And then once you have 100 people in the business, the dynamic changes again. You can still be friends, but no matter how much you might want to, you can't hang out together in the way that you used to. You need to create a bit of distance and separation between you and them.

By the time you reach 400 employees, you may not know all of them by name. But you now have a different concern: you need to become aware of your authority. You need to be conscious of the power that your position within the business carries and the impact that can have on other people.

If I am a bit snappy with some poor kid at work who has maybe never spoken to me before, that is pretty brutal on him. To the wrong person, it can be crushing. So, you have to be careful with what you say, how you say it and to whom, because it carries a lot more weight when you are running a business with 400+ employees than one with 12. Probably more weight than you even imagine.

Know that one day you will need to fire a friend

There will come a time when you have to fire a friend. I have had to do it many times and it is always painful. I agonise over it for days because I know what's going to happen. It is a nightmare, and it never gets any easier, but sadly it has to be done. I have 450 people in the business and I cannot jeopardise their livelihoods by having passengers. I cannot jeopardise my objectivity or my credibility either by having people who are close to me who aren't performing.

Whenever you have to let someone go, I always try to do it quickly and to be as generous as I can without setting a precedence of compensation that I can't keep up.

If ever you find yourself in a life-threatening situation where you need to fire many people to save the company, my best advice is to do the above but to cut deep all in one go. The last thing you want to be doing is making many smaller cuts as it creates a fearful and unsettled environment. So be quick about it, cut deep in one strike and be as generous as you possibly can.

Don't expect people to like you

If you are starting up a business, you can't expect everyone to like you, but, more importantly, you shouldn't try to make everyone like you. If you are always worrying about your employees not liking you, then it will be really hard to run the company.

When former employees write horrible things about me, of course it is upsetting. But I also understand that this is not a popularity contest, so I get over it pretty quickly. One disgruntled ex-employee once wrote, "Christian might think that he is the Wolf of Wall Street, but he is actually the Pony of Pimlico", which is actually pretty funny.

Make it a priority that your business wins popularity contests, rather than you personally. What matters most is that your customers love your business and what it provides for them.

Step 6
Recruit. Recruit. Recruit.

BUSINESSES OFTEN UNDERESTIMATE the importance of recruiting the right people into their various teams. They don't take it nearly seriously enough. In the early days of XLN, I was guilty of doing that too. But recruitment needs to be a key priority because without a continual flow of new high-quality people coming into a business, it will stagnate and eventually slide backwards.

Look beyond the CV

A person's CV tells you almost nothing about them. When you hire someone to work in your business, the three things you need to look for are attitude, passion and hunger. Skills are useful, but having someone who fits the culture of your business is far more important. You can always teach skills, but you cannot teach character or values.

Remember also that a CV is written by the applicant, so they'll obviously try and make it look as rosy as possible. That includes references, which are usually only from people that have nice things to say about the applicant. I hardly ever look at someone's CV, preferring instead to speak to the individual. I am most interested in understanding what makes them tick and hearing stories that illustrate some of the values I'm looking for. The fact that someone volunteers for community work on weekends is super important to know. Likewise, so is that they used to sell lemonade by the roadside as a kid. Try and chat in an informal way that facilitates a relaxed exchange of information that properly reflects the individual's character.

Decide how much experience you actually need

At XLN, we have found that while having relevant experience is obviously important for more senior or technical hires, for salespeople it is actually not that important. In fact, if people come in to XLN with a lot of previous sales experience, it can actually be detrimental.

I would rather have somebody with zero experience than someone with ten years' experience, because I can teach someone with zero experience from day one, whereas somebody with ten years' experience will constantly be saying, "well, in my previous job we used to do it like this". If someone already has experience, it is going to take a lot of effort to get them to a point where I can start showing them the way we do it. Far better to pick someone with the right attitude and then train them up.

Have a constant recruitment policy

Ideally you want to be recruiting all the time because for a business to be successful, it needs a constant flow of fresh blood. Having new people joining the business will invigorate a team and put a very subtle level of pressure on the people who already work for you to improve their performance. That's because if you are constantly recruiting new people, it sends the message to everyone else that if they aren't doing their job properly, then someone else will take their place. It is like being a football manager – if you only have 11 players, then everyone knows they will be playing on Saturday, whether or not they had a poor game last week. But if you have 30 players on the bench, everyone knows that if they don't play a great game tomorrow, they won't get to play the next Saturday.

There is another reason too, particularly for sales teams. You need to recruit continually because otherwise your salespeople will be sitting there thinking, 'there is no end to this, I am going to be here for the next ten years. I am not going anywhere, because they are not promoting anyone, and they are not growing the department.' Not a lot of people want to work in sales for the rest of their lives. Everyone wants to feel that they are getting better and progressing in their career, no matter what they do.

If your business is running well, the people you recruit should be getting better and being promoted, so you will need to constantly feed the machine.

Fit the process to the position

Salespeople always interview brilliantly, so don't waste time putting them through three or four interviews – it will not achieve anything. Instead, put them to work so you can see them in action. If they show that they don't have the values or performance that you are looking for, get rid of them.

Sometimes you will want to have a very wide-door recruitment policy, as outlined above, but other times you might need the exact opposite. For example, if you are looking for a senior software architect. In that case, you need to determine the applicant's technical ability and their suitability within your team or department. That makes for a very different recruitment process and hence, you need to adapt. Different strokes for different folks.

Hire fast, fire faster - promote even faster.

One aspect of recruitment and development of people I have learnt again and again is that you should hire fast. If a person seems right and has what you are looking for, then get on with it and hire them.

Good people don't hang around and they get hired by your competition if you procrastinate. Another really important thing to get comfortable with is that if a person isn't working out or they just don't seem to fit with your company culture, you must fire them even faster than you hired them.

Wrong hires don't improve with time, quite the contrary. My final and critical piece of advice on this subject is: when you realise that you have hired a good one and they are performing and thriving, promote them immediately.

This is all part of the process of finding and developing great people. The cream rises to the top and you have to create an environment where progression and promotion is visible to all and the reward for putting forward the right behaviours.

Get the right balance

When you are trying to put together a team, it can be useful to maintain a balance between the kinds of people you are recruiting. For the team dynamics to work, you want a good balance of characters and a good balance of men and women. Age doesn't really matter, but it does matter that people look smart and presentable. Being well dressed shows that they respect the job you are giving them, and they respect your business and what it stands for. I also find that well-dressed salespeople tend to have more confidence and thus perform better. As Mark Twain said, "clothes make the man".

Do the recruitment yourself

We don't use external recruiters because they are not as passionate about our business as we are. You have got to be enthusiastic about what you do, and somebody who does the recruitment for 15 different companies cannot possibly complete the task with the same energy and rigour as we can.

At XLN, we have a whole team that deals with recruitment on a daily basis, and we measure what it is achieving multiple times a day so that we are sure that we always have a consistent number of quality people coming into the business.

Don't just stick to the usual recruitment methods

It is very difficult to hire great high-level managers and directors, so many businesses resort to hiring a head-hunter to do a search and get lots of references. They then present you with three or four possible candidates to interview, and once your team has met them all, you put them through psychometric tests. And if they pass all of that, then you might hire them. Frankly though, it's a 50/50 coin toss whether it works out. It is a bit like speed dating – people may look the part and say all the right things, but it is not a true reflection of who they really are.

I have found that it is much better to cast the net wider and consider people who may not even be looking for a new job. If you meet someone at a dinner who is a sales director and you really like them and think that you could work with them, then keep in touch. Follow their company and their individual progress and look at the results they achieve over a period of time. You can also meet up with them for lunch occasionally. Then, when the timing feels right, you can invite them to join the business and offer them a salary and incentive package that they can't say no to. This is a much better way of doing recruitment and works a million times better than the head-hunter route, in my opinion.

And if you happen to find someone who you think would be fantastic for your business who is immediately available, hire them regardless. Don't bother waiting for there to be a specific need, you will find something for them to do. The right people pretty much always come along at the wrong time. They certainly never turn up when you need them, so you need to get them when you find them. That's why you should always be recruiting – never stop looking for great people that fit your company culture.

Shake the tree

When you manage a team of people you will find from time to time that some of them will seem to fade. There can be many reasons for this, but clearly having unmotivated, unproductive or disengaged people employed is a bad thing for your team and business. The way I deal with this is akin to shaking a tree with the view to finding out whether the 'bushbaby' is going to hold on or fall out.

The conversation goes a bit like this: "How are things going? How do you feel about your career and your progress? I've noticed that lately you seem less engaged and I was wondering whether we were coming to the end of the road here?"

Once that bomb has landed you stay quiet. Now, one of two things is going to happen, and in a way both are positive. Either the employee clings to the tree branch and says something like: "No, no, no. I love my job and love working here, but I've been distracted because of…" Or they say something along the lines of: "Well, I've been thinking and…"

Either way you both win. If the employee is still fired up about their job and career then great – you've both reaffirmed your commitment to the future. If not, then it's time for them to exit and you've shortened the time the employee would have lingered unproductive in the business.

This is a positive thing to do and should be conducted in a supportive and empathetic way, with the view of ensuring the employee is in the right job or company. If something is getting in the way of that objective, then you can discuss it and work to solve the problem together.

Step 7
Provide Amazing Customer Service

GOOD CUSTOMER SERVICE is not just something that is nice to have, it is absolutely essential, especially for our customers. As small-business owners, they are completely dependent on us to solve problems when things go wrong.

Most of the high street is made up of small businesses such as hairdressers, restaurants, small shops and cafés. If their phone or broadband goes down, they cannot take bookings or orders, and if their card machine goes down, they cannot take payments.

Such businesses are often living hand to mouth – if they can't take payments and lose half a day's trading because only half of their potential customers have cash on them, they will seriously feel it. In this situation, some could even go out of business. We take good customer service seriously because our customers do. And no matter what kind of business you set up, you must too.

This is how to do it right.

Answer the phone quickly

There is nothing more frustrating than calling a business to ask for help and then hearing a recorded message telling you that you are in a queue. These messages often say, "your call is important to us", but clearly it isn't because otherwise they would have answered the phone straightaway. We answer all of our calls in six seconds on average, and they are answered by a human being who speaks English and who cares about the customer's business.

We don't make our customers press buttons or key in their phone number, we just answer the phone promptly and ask how we can help. We don't want to make life any more complicated than it needs to be.

Empower your employees to fix the problem even if it is outside their remit

If you are a medium-sized business, you may be able to employ technical support, but if you are a small business, it's usually just you – and you, like me, probably wouldn't know one end of an Ethernet cable from the other.

We train our customer service representatives to do whatever it takes to solve the problem our customers are facing, and to do it in a calm and patient matter. In fact, around 90% of the problems our customers contact us about are solved by the initial person they speak to. More importantly, they are solved during that first phone call. We always try to fix the problem, even if it is not something we are responsible for, like a printer. Anything to get their business up and running again. That is the kind of customer service that really makes a difference.

Make it easy for customers to get in touch

Give your customers lots of different ways to contact you so that they can choose the one that is easiest for them. Don't make your customers fill out an online form or send an email if all they want to do is pick up the phone. And if English isn't their first language, they can speak to one of our many employees who speak other languages, such as Urdu, Punjabi, Chinese, and Turkish.

Build enduring relationships

At XLN, we have learnt to do marketing by not doing marketing. By this, I mean that we have never spent any money on newspaper or TV advertising, or brochures for prospective customers. Instead, we devote all our efforts to building relationships with prospective customers, so that they will naturally want to get in touch.

There are two reasons we take this approach. First, when I was running a small business, I instinctively disliked – and ignored – all the traditional kinds of marketing. I used to chuck brochures and leaflets in the bin. Second, because I realised that building relationships is a much more effective way to stay close to your customers. In fact, we don't just see our customers as customers, we regard them as long-term partners.

Think about how you can do this in your business. Think how you would treat your best friend when they ask for help, and treat your customers that very same way.

Letter To My Son Milo

A S I STARTED to write this book, my son Milo was only 9 years old. He has now just turned 11 – that's because I've sat on this manuscript for quite a while. I'm not sure he has much interest in what his daddy does at work and I don't blame him for that. Life as a 9–11-year-old is pretty full on with school and other activities.

I also can't be certain that, by the time he develops an interest, I'll still be around or that I will be able to remember all the lessons I learnt during my business career.

So, I thought I'd put down on paper what I wished I would have known when I was starting out in business and in the real world. Obviously, some of the points that follow will have been covered at some point in the preceding chapters, so I apologise for the repetition.

Make sure you love what you do

Very often the things you love doing and the areas where you are talented are the same. Talent only gets you so far though, it's hard work and practice that makes up the other 90%. Unless you pick a job, role or career that you love, the hard work and relentless practice will quickly become dreary and eventually you will quit.

If, like me, you pick a career you truly love, then you will never work a single day in your life because you spend your time doing something you love. It's like playing with your favourite toys all day long.

Don't be impatient

Don't ever rush things – it won't produce good results. Take your time and make sure you do whatever it is well the first-time round. I remember being too impatient to join the Queens Guard after leaving school and I always regretted that. It really wouldn't have made any difference whether I started my entrepreneurial career one or two years later. In hindsight, it wouldn't have mattered whether I got to my current position two years later either.

Remember it is a forever game we are playing. The only thing that really matters is that you are loving the journey and enjoying the game.

Pick the right life partner

This is a really important one and I was very lucky with Mamma. No matter the journey you set out on, you will probably want to settle down and get married. Choosing the right person will be one of the most critical decisions of your life. Make sure you choose someone you respect deeply and someone you have common interests with.

Mamma and I decided very early on in our relationship that we wouldn't try to change anything about each other. In other words, we would accept the other, warts and all. The brilliance of that decision was that we have never argued about all the little things that often drive couples mad. Clearly, I'm not perfect. And there are many things that I do which irritate Mamma. But because we made that agreement, you have never seen Mamma criticise me for any of my many flaws.

If you accept someone 100% for who they are and not for who you'd like them to be, it will make for a harmonious family life.

Never spend more than you earn

The reason many people end up poor is because they consistently spend more money than they earn. Never do that – if you can't afford something, don't buy it. Ever.

There is a big difference between what you need and what you want. Only spend money on things you need and always buy quality. Even though quality is more expensive, it will work out cheaper in the long run. A great handmade pair of shoes will last you 20 years if you look after them. They may be more expensive than the fast fashion of the day, but they will last a long time. And if you add up the cost of the many pairs you would've thrown away over the years, you come out quids in.

The only thing that is worse than being poor is being old and poor, so always try to save money.

The rule of 72

This is one of the most important things to understand about money and investing. When you invest your money, you earn a return either in interest or as a capital gain. This is calculated as a percentage annually. The rule of 72 is all about compound interest and is one of the most overlooked areas of long-term investing. If you divide 72 by your annual return, say 8%, then you get nine. If the return is 12%, then 72 divided by 12 is six.

What that means is that if you earn 8% per year on the money you have invested, then the total doubles every nine years. If you earn 12%, then your total invested wealth doubles every six years.

As a result, I encourage everyone to start investing or saving as soon as possible. For example, if you invested £10,000 when you are 35 years old and earn 10% per year in annual return, by the time you are 56 years old the total would have increased to £80,000.

In this case, the rule of 72 means that your money would double every 7.2 years. In the first 7.2-year period you would accumulate £20,000; in the second you would reach £40,000; and in the third you would reach £80,000. By age 56, 21.6 years after investing £10,000, your money would have increased eight times.

Invest wisely, don't take huge risk and be patient. Over the long term you'll get rich.

Develop great habits

You form habits and then they form you. Figure out which habits are critical to your success and then consciously work at developing them. It usually takes about three weeks to develop a habit, regardless of whether it is a good or bad one.

Make sure you develop good and successful habits in all parts of your life. If, like me, you have an obsessive-compulsive nature, you will have to be extra vigilant about your bad habits. Make sure you surround yourself with good mates that can tell you honestly when you are going off track. If that were to happen, make sure you talk to the right people about it and seek help if you can't fix it on your own.

Don't worry about what people think

We all want to be liked and loved by the people around us. That's just a natural instinct. But the reality is that no matter who you are and how you act, someone will still dislike you. So you can't win the game of 'everybody love me' – there is no point even trying.

Be yourself and stay true to that; some people will like you and some won't. Don't worry about that. The most important thing is that you like yourself and that will only happen if you do things that are likeable in your own eyes. From my experience, you are a wonderful, very loveable boy and I love you very much.

Be grateful and have faith

In AA meetings, members recite a great saying called the Serenity Prayer, which I use a lot. It goes: "Grant me the serenity to accept the things I cannot change, courage to change the things I can, and wisdom to know the difference".

It's important to be grateful for the things you have in your life; don't ever worry about the things you don't have. We have all been blessed with so many wonderful gifts and it's critical to focus on those and all the good stuff in your life. Be grateful for the small things and make it a habit to count your blessings on a daily basis.

Stay fit and learn some great social games

This is a lesson I'm learning a bit too late in my life. Being active is incredibly important, particularly as you get older. You are already an accomplished gymnast, so I'm hoping you will continue to stay fit throughout your life. If you develop those habits early, then I am convinced you can have a wonderfully active life right up into your 80s. If you don't stay fit, your quality of life will start diminishing from the age of 50 or 60. Don't make that mistake.

Also, as I have no doubt told you before, you should learn some of the great social games, like tennis, golf, cricket, football, skiing or sailing. It doesn't really matter which sports you decide on. By participating, you will open up a new social circle of friends that will give you much pleasure throughout your life. As you know, if daddy didn't have his golf, he would probably have gone insane. Other hobbies, regardless of what they may be, are also important. In an ideal world, you would share some of these hobbies and sports with your life partner.

Good manners

'Manners maketh man' is the motto for both Winchester College and New College, Oxford. I think this is somewhat true.

Certainly, good manners are incredibly important, even if they aren't valued as much today as they were when I was a kid. And as I have often told you, I think good manners and playing some social sports well is perhaps even more important than excelling in school. Good manners will take you far in life and open doors to you, whereas academic prowess will only get you started on a career path. Don't get me wrong, I'm not belittling school or your top grades, but I'm just saying that manners are super important and you should develop them just like any other great habit you will need in your long life.

Don't chase fame

Fame is not something to aspire to. I have known some very famous people, Mamma even more so, and one thing I have realised is that it is not nearly as attractive as it might seem. If you become famous by virtue of your job or your accomplishments, then that's fine. But don't go chasing fame, because it brings with it a hollow and lonely world.

You won't be able to walk anonymously down the street or through an airport, you won't be able to have dinner in a public restaurant, and your private life will be constantly splashed across newspapers and online. It isn't what you think it might be and should be avoided at all costs. Anonymity and privacy should be treasured.

Start a family relatively young

At the end of the day, whether you become rich or not, your family will be the most valuable thing in your life. And as you become older, you will long to have them around as much as possible. Sadly, Mamma and I only had two children. We are very grateful for both you and Theo, but we would have loved more children. We simply started a bit too late. Please don't make the same mistake.

Children always come at an inconvenient moment. There is never a perfect time. Having said that, the earlier you have kids, the more energy you have to play with them. And being slightly younger means that you have the opportunity to have a fair few if that is what you and your life partner would like. If I could change anything in my life, I would have had children earlier, in my early 30s.

Don't be afraid to take risks

Life is not a spectator sport – you need to get stuck in. That means taking risks, but only the calculated ones. If you know the subject matter well and have confidence in your abilities, then work out the probability of success and take a calculated gamble. If the odds are any less than 70% in your favour, you might as well go to a casino and put your money on red. Only take a risk if you are confident that it will work out in your favour. Improve your odds by studying new subjects, practising your skills and preparing yourself for battle.

On the subject of battles, you need to pick yours carefully. What that means is that you can't fight every battle that comes your way. Hence, you need to pick the ones that really matter to you. If it is not important to you, then don't fight the battle.

Buy yourself a great place to live and make it a home

There is no right or wrong way to do this. However, the way I was brought up, and the way you have seen your Mamma and I live, a great family home has always been important to us. My first priority was always to get a nice home. My advice: buy the best house you can afford in the best area.

I always felt that I would rather have a great home than buy fancy cars or go on expensive holidays. If you only own one house, then you are not invested in property. After all, it is your home, and you will get pleasure from it every day of your life. So don't worry about whether house prices go up or down. If they go up, the next house you buy will be equally expensive; if prices drop, the next one will be cheaper.

Your mortgage should be such that you can pay for it under all circumstances. Paying the mortgage should always be your number-one priority, because otherwise you might lose the house one day.

Your dear brother Theo

You have been such a wonderful brother to Theo. I can only imagine how difficult it must have been for you to have a brother with special needs. At times, you must have felt that all of our attention was on Theo and I'm really sorry if that upset you. As a parent, you always tend to protect the weaker one and I know that isn't fair, but I hope you understand and can forgive us.

It is impossible to predict what will happen with Theo as the years go by, but please don't ever feel like it is up to you to look after him. You have your life to live, and Theo mustn't get in the way of that. There will be some very difficult decisions to make in the future but that is for us to worry about and not you. I have no doubt that Theo couldn't want for a better brother and he loves you very much. Don't ever doubt that.

You are a wonderful, caring and loving boy. You have a great mind and have been given a great physique, so you owe it to yourself to take advantage of that. I love you very very much and have been so proud of all your accomplishments so far, be they academic, artistic or physical. I really couldn't be any prouder as a father and I know you will go far and create a wonderful life for yourself and your family. I only hope I will be here to witness it all unfold. Trust your instincts and don't be afraid to love the people close to you.

You are my greatest creation and I know you will change the world for the better.

I will love you always and be there for you whenever you need me.

Your devoted and loving father.

The Deal That
Wasn't To Be

A S I'VE BEEN writing this book, time has flown by and a number of things have happened that I thought I should include for the sake of completeness.

Towards the end of 2018 and in the early months of 2019, it became clear to me that I had lost my enthusiasm for the business. Almost 20 years of hard slog and organic growth had finally taken its toll – I felt burnt out and uninspired. I couldn't see XLN's future direction clearly and had lost my hunger and drive. It pains me to write, but that was the honest truth.

Lacking in motivation, I considered leaving XLN.

Something that played a key part in my deliberations was that my CFO, Neil Conaghan, was increasingly keen on running the business without me involved. It is very natural for ambitious and smart people to want to run their own show, and Neil had often said that it was his ambition to one day run his own shop. Perhaps this was the right time.

I took no personal offence to this – you have to understand that if you hire ambitious people, they will ultimately have their eye on your job. I was, however, slightly concerned, because running a business can seem very easy when you are watching an accomplished leader do it.

The stars aligned and in late January 2019, I agreed with Frank, our chairman, that we should allow Neil to lead a private-equity-backed MBO (management buy-out). I also discussed it with my investor, GSO, and they were supportive provided we could get a fair price for the business.

I told Neil what I had decided and what my terms were. Broadly speaking, my terms were a sensible valuation of around ten times current run-rate profitability, 100% cash out, no roll with very limited warranties, and no involvement going forward. I also wanted certain provisions for select individuals in the organisation, including assurances of job security.

The first step was a beauty parade of potential advisors, which included Rothschild, Lazard, and Arma Partners. We eventually hired Lazard to lead the sale process and started the customary work of due diligence in all the relevant areas such as financial, legal and commercial, as well as preparing the information memorandum (IM), which is the sales book sent to all prospective buyers.

The IM went out to about a dozen prospective buyers, mainly from the private-equity community, and first round bids were expected in mid-June. We received a good number of bids in the range we expected which were, as always, subject to due diligence. We selected five bidders and they were all sent the due diligence work in order for them to firm up their offers.

Neil and the senior-management team then started meeting with the private-equity firms that had made it through to the second round. Normally I would have been heavily involved in this process, but we had decided that I would not be present at these meetings. The reason being, of course, that if I was present and played a key role in these meetings, the potential buyer might get the brilliant idea that they wanted me to remain a part of the running of the company. Not only did I not want to do that, but I also felt that it would be impossible for Neil to flourish if he continued to be in my shadow. It's a known fact that being CEO in a company where the founder and major shareholder is still around is a nightmare.

When the second-round bids came in, following the management presentations and due diligence work, alarm bells started ringing for me. The bids were all towards the lower end of the range that had been indicated in round one. Usually, you would expect offers to be towards the higher end, if not occasionally above. It was starting to become clear to me that the business was being pitched at a too conservative level and the buyers didn't see enough potential upside to get really excited. A few buyers pulled out and we declined a few, which left us with just two: Equistone and TowerBrook Capital Partners.

TowerBrook is not known for paying top prices, but to be fair to them, they are also a bit too big for the size of XLN. They usually try to invest a minimum of £100m and then have the opportunity to put more money to work. That pretty much ruled them out.

That left us with Equistone and their London team, who made us an offer. It just so happened that Neil was old mates with the chap leading the investment, Tim Swales. I had been assured that this wouldn't be an issue though, and should actually have facilitated a smooth transaction. It was by now obvious that Neil, not maliciously, had pitched the business from a safety-first point of view. Essentially, he was telling investors that if XLN just carried on doing what we had been doing for years and nothing exciting happened, then they would still make 2–3 times their money. But he hadn't included any real upside or blue-sky thinking such as transformational M&A, which could turbocharge the returns and deliver 4–5 times their money.

That was a big mistake, in hindsight, and we set about changing that. We agreed on a supplementary presentation outlining all the exciting initiatives that we could and should pursue, but frankly it was too late.

Once a private-equity house gets a purchase price stuck in their head, all their actions are focused on backing into that number – it is virtually impossible to change their minds. It is also my firm belief that they genuinely thought I would budge and take their offer, even though I had made it clear that it wasn't a fair reflection of the company's value and I wouldn't sell at that price.

What so often happens is that a founder says that they won't ever sell for less than £X. A private-equity house then puts a cheque on the table of 60% of X and the founder takes it after realising that it will change their life – they usually decide that they can happily live without the other 40%

That was Tim Swales' first mistake. He probably calculated that if he put £40m in front of me, that I would take it. Little did he consider that I was already financially independent and didn't need the money. My point was one of principle. I wasn't willing to sell on the cheap because it would have serious implications for my other shareholders, particularly all my employee shareholders who would suffer a significant reduction in the value of their stakes.

I told Neil that I wouldn't sell at the terms Equistone had offered and that we should stop the sale process and get back to work. I then went away to the south of France with my wife Naima and our youngest son Milo for two weeks. During that period, Neil continued to negotiate with Tim and eventually came up with a deal construct that I could just about live with. So I agreed to sell.

By the time the two weeks were up and we were looking to head home, Tim Swales made his second, terminal mistake. He had started playing around with the terms of the deal we had agreed. Normally, private-equity houses are very protective of their reputations as future deal flow depends on them maintaining a good standing in the market place. I can only speculate as to why Equistone decided to alter our terms, but certainly it was disappointing and I must say one of the very few disagreeable experiences I've had with private equity.

You live and learn though, and I had my part to play in the failed sale process. I'll chalk this down to expensive school fees – a sale process like this cost something in the neighbourhood of £1m. Ouch.

Neil was mortified and very apologetic when he caught me on the phone in the BA departure lounge of Nice airport. To be fair to Neil, he advised me not to sell at the price and terms that Tim had offered. We agreed that he should tell Tim in no uncertain terms that the deal was off and that I didn't want anything more to do with him.

Sometimes you find yourself in situations that just don't make any sense. The price I had agreed to sell at was incredibly attractive and would have made Equistone, Neil, and my other employee shareholders a lot of money over the following years. But for some reason, Tim ensured that it wasn't to be.

Once back in London, Tim insisted we meet so he could explain the deal construct in more detail. I reluctantly agreed and took the meeting.

"Now that we know each other better, I really think we could do a lot of great things together going forward" were the final words I registered Tim saying as I replied: "the fact that we know each other better is a really bad thing" and showed him the door.

As the deal was unravelling during the final weeks of August, Neil had commented that he didn't want to go back to his previous role of Group CFO now that he had straddled the CEO post for a while. So when I returned to the office in early September, I called him into my office and fired him.

Screwing up deals like these have consequences.

Biggest Curveball
In History

FOLLOWING MY RETURN to the business in September 2019, it became clear that there was still a lot of interest in the company from private-equity investors. By January 2020, we had received two or three offers that were superior to the Equistone bid, but I decided to turn them all down and commit to another chapter in the history of XLN.

After my 'chat' with Neil in early September, we subsequently had a few more discussions. It became pretty clear that Neil had taken quite a beating during the sale process and was rather shell-shocked afterwards. He made it clear that he didn't want to leave XLN and was willing to go back to being Group CFO if that was what I wanted him to do. At no point had I lost confidence in Neil and not for a second did I think that he had been trying to be even the slightest bit underhand, so I allowed him to return to his position of CEO. We all make mistakes and I felt he had learnt some valuable lessons.

It has always been my philosophy in life that it's all about playing the hand you've been dealt in the best way possible. No point in crying over a few weak cards or hoping that something will magically change. No, in my mind, it's all about playing a situation optimally. And to be fair, the leadership team we have at XLN is about as good as it gets. It's not perfect, but probably a nine out of ten. But after the upheaval of the failed sale, it was time for a change.

I wanted to redefine the role I played in XLN. I had been in charge as CEO for pretty much all of my career and, to be honest, I had become bored of micromanaging and making sure that stuff got done. I've never claimed to be the best people manager – I'm far too impatient, intolerant at times, and my expectations for myself and anyone around me are way too high – but I never felt I could let go because I feared things would fall apart and I'd end up back at square one again.

In Neil, Saeed Sheikh and Panny Koullas, along with the rest of the senior team, I have all the capabilities I could ever wish for. It was just a matter of figuring out how to harness and shepherd those talents in the right way. We agreed that Neil would stay on as CEO and everyone else would keep their respective roles. The main change would be that I would be the 'armchair quarterback' and direct the business without getting too involved in the day-to-day management. I would set the overall strategy, be involved in the product selection, and design and agree the pricing strategy. And then be more hands-on in corporate culture, the customer experience and designing the sales channels. But all from a distance, as I didn't want to get in the way of my executive team and confuse staff over who they reported to.

Now I just needed to find my mojo again and get fired up. That was to prove harder than I first anticipated.

Life intervened, as it so often does, and in late January, the news started reporting a virus taking hold in Wuhan, China. By early March, countries across Europe, such as my birthplace Denmark, had decided to lock down their economies and citizens in order to prevent the virus spreading.

Suddenly, it was everyone to their battle stations and all hands on deck. Saeed, my trusted COO, had already upgraded all our systems to allow for remote working, so within two days of the government locking down the country we had every single customer-facing employee working from home. I made the decision to fire all our sales staff, as they wouldn't be able to operate – it was now a question of saving the company. We drew down all credit facilities we had access to and spoke to GSO, who agreed an interest and repayment holiday to conserve cash. In all, we managed to scrounge together the best part of £11m in cash, which I was hopeful would see us through. Luckily, the Chancellor announced his furlough scheme, meaning we could keep our sales channels alive but dormant. I reduced all senior management salaries, and our chairman and I took a 100% cut.

Now that the company was in a shape that I hoped would see us through, we started turning our attention to how we could best support and help our small-business customers. It was pretty obvious that if small businesses were forced to close, they wouldn't be needing their internet connection or phone system for a period of time and they desperately needed to save as much cash as they possibly could.

Initially, we tried to work with the industry to come up with an industry-wide solution whereby we could suspend connections and hence save them their monthly subscriptions. Disappointingly, it quickly became clear that if this was ever going to happen, it would take too long to implement – the damage might have been done by the time BT and others got their act together.

So, we bit the bullet and offered our customers free call diverts to wherever they wanted their business calls to be re-routed to. We also reduced tariffs to a level our customers were happy with and able to pay. We suspended accounts completely and all the while kept answering the phone, in person, within an average of six seconds. It was costing us a fortune every month, but the goal was to try and come out the other end with as many customers alive as humanly possible, regardless of the short-term cost. To be fair, and to give credit where credit is due, one of our main suppliers, TalkTalk, stepped up to the plate and helped admirably in this regard.

We started losing customers in huge numbers and I feared for the viability of the company. April and May were horrendous, as we had no new sales coming in, but we took the decision in June to start mobilising our sales channels again so that we could hit the ground running once the lockdown was over. We started designing a new connectivity product that would allow our customers to work partly from home but with the same quality connection and service levels they were used to in their business.

As soon as the lockdown was over, it was full steam ahead. Terry Fitzgerald, my brilliant, newly-promoted sales director, and myself started travelling the country getting the sales guys fired up. July, August (normally a poor sales month because of holidays), September and October saw huge sales numbers and growth. For the first time since I effectively stepped down in late 2018, we had net customer growth and were on fire with annual net subscriber growth of 6%.

God, I love a good crisis.

It is during tough times you see what people are made of. For example, during this time I could clearly see who we could count on and who had stepped up. Likewise, it becomes pretty obvious who isn't a team player and only has their own interests at heart. I took this opportunity to rid the business of those individuals and slim the company down in preparation for future growth.

I think that, during a crisis, it is really important for a leader to do the five following things:

1. Be visible and lead by example.

2. Communicate clearly and consistently.

3. Be calm and decisive while looking for solutions.

4. Show empathy and be supportive.

5. Focus on your employees and your customers.

Nobody knows, as I write, when this pandemic will be over, but with a number of successful vaccines available, I hope it won't be too long. Once the dust settles and the damage becomes evident, I can only hope that our customers and UK businesses as a whole will rise from the ashes and thrive again.

No doubt irreparable damage will have been done to our high streets and business fabric, but we will adapt and change and prosper anew.

That I have no doubt about. The resilience of UK small businesses is astounding and sometimes we need a shock like this to make the changes that are necessary for a new and exciting future, which I'm convinced is beckoning over the horizon.

What's Next
The Future of XLN

DURING THE SUMMER of 2020, we decided to get XLN's refinancing done. Back in the final months of 2014, we had done a deal with GSO that allowed us to exit ECI Partners and take control of the company. ECI had made three times their money and were very happy with their investment in XLN. The only slight niggle was that we owed GSO £115m, which was high leverage at 7.5 times EBITDA.

The GSO debt was a seven-year bullet loan that was coming to expiry in November 2021, so now was as good a time as any to refinance. Miraculously, we have managed to navigate the Covid crisis of 2020 with almost no perceptible financial impact and that's saying something given that we posted our best ever financial results at the end of March 2020 at £21.4m EBITDA.

GSO, now Blackstone Credit, owned 30% of the company and our net debt was roughly £85m. On top of that, management had a chunk of preference shares, or loan notes, in the business. We hired advisors to help us manage the refinancing process but, as the cliché goes, it actually turned out to be me doing the deal on the golf course.

I had met Mike Dennis, partner and co-head of European Credit at Ares Management Corporation, some time ago and we had discussed the possibility of him refinancing the business. We restarted the conversation during lockdown and as soon as we were allowed outside again, we set up a game of golf at Sunningdale Golf Club. By the time we were halfway up the second fairway we had agreed a deal, a real partnership approach, in principle.

The deal was completed on 18 December; Mike lent the business £125.7m and took a 15% equity stake as well. We managed to get a good exit for GSO, who have been an absolute dream to work with, and I truly hope to work with them again in the future. A huge thanks to Mike Whitman and particularly Mike Carruthers, Leopold Walde, and the rest of the GSO team.

We are now looking forward to creating something really big and successful. And we've got just the way to do it.

One of the unexpected benefits of writing this book, re-reading it, and finally finishing it during this funky pandemic period, is that I've had to re-acquaint myself with the lessons and habits that got me here in the first place.

When I started my journey as an entrepreneur, I was just a 22-year-old kid in Mile End who set himself some really big goals. I've largely achieved those goals now and along the way I've also realised some other childhood dreams, like building my own home. You have now read the journey I've been on, or at least some of it, and I hope some of the points I've made will help you on your way.

As you know, I lost my mojo and found it really hard to get inspired and motivated about work again. Well, I've just realised why. It's because I had pretty much reached all my goals and hadn't been able to find a new one to get excited about. But now I have. It suddenly occurred to me as I was writing that I hadn't consciously set myself a really big, worthwhile and inspiring stretch goal for a long time. And importantly, one that I could visualise us achieving; one that I could see a clear path towards.

Our next goal is to turn XLN into a £1bn (that's right, one billion pound) company in the next 4–5 years. Now that's a goal that can get my juices flowing. I'm fired up about it and so is the rest of the management team. Particularly since we can see a clear and shining path of how to get there.

This is how we are going to do it.

Start with the end

We've got a business that makes roughly £20m a year and has decent, organic, net-subscriber growth of 6% annually.

The next step, which we have already started on, is to get the business into great shape. We need to grow our existing sales channels by 25% and improve all aspects of our operation. This includes possible changes to the management structure and further development of our customer-service and product portfolio.

To make the company worth £1bn, we need to be making around £60m in EBITDA. To achieve that through organic growth is very hard and will take a long time though, so we are instead embarking on an acquisition spree. In other words, we want to buy other companies that are similar to XLN and put them together. The two overriding considerations here are that the customer focus of the target companies must be similarly concentrated on the small end of the SME (small and medium-sized enterprise) market and that the product set must be complementary.

We've identified 4–5 companies in our industry that are ripe for acquisition and consolidation, and these businesses are all sized between £10m and £30m in EBITDA.

The UK telecoms market is very fragmented and so we should be able to find enough targets to pursue. The pandemic and potential future capital-gains tax increases are likely to make owners think seriously about selling out in the next few years too.

Assuming we can buy these companies for a maximum of nine or ten times their earnings and can integrate them efficiently, then we should be able to extract synergies of 40–50% of their level of profitability. If we can't achieve that, we simply won't buy them and will look for other targets to acquire.

Once we reach our profitability goal of £60m, I'm pretty confident that we can float XLN on the stock exchange. If we have decent growth, I think a price-to-earnings (P/E) ratio of 15 is realistic – particularly in the current low-interest-rate environment. Once listed, the business should be able to deliver dividend returns of more than 6% annually. And at a valuation of £1bn, that's a very attractive prospect from an investment point of view.

Here's the beautiful part. Because we've got a great debt provider in Ares, who have very deep pockets (£7.5bn at last count) and are a shareholder in XLN, we are able to borrow six times our EBITDA at a relatively low interest rate of around 7% per annum.

So, if we buy a business with £15m in EBITDA for £135m (nine times their earnings) and we can extract synergies of, say, £7.5m, then we can borrow six times £22.5m to cover the £135m cost. In essence, we need to find two companies of that size with the right characteristics for us to reach £60m in EBITDA. We will have some organic growth on top of that too, so there should be room to spare, which is always prudent to plan for.

Of course, there are fees and sometimes I'm sure the maths won't quite stack up, but we should have a bit of EBITDA in reserve once we have paid down some debt from the refinancing.

I know it sounds easy, but obviously it won't be – there will undoubtedly be many obstacles along the road that we need to overcome. And from a financial point of view, it will be tight, and we may well have to sell some equity to make it all happen. But the most important thing is that you can see a clear path and, critically, believe in your ability to follow it and achieve your goal.

The next steps are to assemble the necessary team members, if you don't already have them on board, and plan out the work.

Organic growth versus mergers and acquisitions

The biggest obstacles to us achieving our £1bn goal are the variables I have assumed, such as gaining a P/E ratio of 15, organic growth of 10% annually, and synergies of 40–50%.

To achieve a P/E ratio of 15, we must create a sales machine that can achieve organic growth of at least 10% per year. In regard to the synergies, that's a bit easier, as if we can't see ourselves extracting that level of synergies, then we should just walk away and look for another target. If the synergies are there, then it's a question of planning the integration and then executing that plan religiously. You have to be disciplined here and not get swept away by greed, ego or over confidence.

It really boils down to us finding a new way to get customers at such a scale that the customer base grows by at least 10% a year – no small feat. If we can do that, then the rest is achievable. On the other hand, if we can't achieve that goal, the customer base will diminish every year and the business will plateau or even start going backwards. That won't warrant a P/E ratio of 15, so our only option is to find a way to grow in a huge way.

As I've explained, XLN has predominantly grown by using direct sales such as online search, outbound telesales and field sales. We can scale these channels a fair bit, but not enough to replenish the much larger absolute number of naturally churning customers.

So what's a girl to do?

Well, last time I was faced with such a massive conundrum, the brothers and I locked ourselves in the boardroom until we figured out a way to get to 100,000 customers. That way won't work again, but the method is the same – accept no defeat and keep at it until you find a way, or multiple ways, to get to where you want to be. It's the journey of solving the problems that are ultimately the rewarding part, not reaching the goal and trousering the spondoolies.

One thing we have never done before is advertise our business on a grander scale. But as I write, that's what we are contemplating. I had a super exciting Zoom meeting with a fantastic advertising agency just this morning. We are going to give that a try and no doubt you will see some of these ads in the future when they air on social media, digital channels and maybe even TV.

So look out for them in the second half of 2021 and watch this space.

It is going to be one hell of a ride.

Acknowledgements

I dedicate this book to my wonderful mum, Bente Birgitte Nellemann, who sadly passed away much too soon. You taught and showed me so many of the softer qualities and were a constant pillar of support and understanding in my life. I miss you dreadfully and think of you every single day.

My thanks to all the wonderful, hard-working and supportive colleagues I have had the pleasure of working with over the years.

To Kerry Brunson and Billy Reynolds (RIP), who taught me great work habits and supported and shaped me in my early career.

My oldest friend, Henrik Praesius, who believed in me when I didn't believe in myself and has stood by my side since we were 11 years old. Your support gave me the strength and confidence I needed.

My dear friend, Mark Milln, who I met 24 years ago and who's helped me in so many ways.

The Brothers, without whom Euroffice and XLN wouldn't have happened. The three-way partnership we had was one of the best and most inventive and productive times of my life.

Tony Fitzpatrick, who is one of the best people I have ever worked with. I couldn't have built XLN without his constant help, support and friendship. There literally wasn't an operational problem he couldn't solve.

Frank McKay, my current chairman and very close friend. Thank you for all your wisdom, support and guidance. You are without a doubt the best 'operator' I have ever met and you have taught me so much.

The three private-equity firms, Palatine, ECI Partners and Blackstone Credit, I've worked with so far and the partners I have dealt with on a regular basis. Tony Dickin, Gary Tipper, Tom Wrenn, Sean

Whelan, Mike Whitman and Mike Carruthers – a huge thanks for all the support you gave me and the faith you had in me.

Paul Glassberg, my trusted lawyer, who has held my hand through many challenging transactions and periods.

Most of all, my huge thanks to this place – London and the UK – a heaving melting pot of wonderfully industrious and inspiring people. A massively diverse and liberal society built and maintained by people from all nationalities and backgrounds, who largely came from somewhere else and within a generation or two adopted that unique British spirit.

My wife Naima, the love of my life, who encourages and supports me every single day.

If you enjoyed this book, I would be very grateful if you would write a review.

I know I'm asking a lot and it can be a royal pain, but they really do help and they are greatly appreciated.

Thank you.